COMPASSION And COMMAND

How New Managers Master People, Problems, and Performance

BILL AULT

COMPASSION AND COMMAND

HOW NEW MANAGERS MASTER PEOPLE, PROBLEMS, AND PERFORMANCE

BILL AULT

ISBN 978-1-962729-11-6

PUBLISHED IN THE UNITED STATES OF AMERICA BY BOOKNOLOGY, AN ADDUCENT NONFICTION IMPRINT.

BOOK◆NOL◆O◆GY
n. delivering useable information and knowledge
that adds value to people's lives

ADDUCENT, INC.
JACKSONVILLE, FLORIDA
WWW.ADDUCENTCREATIVE.COM

CONTENTS

PART 1: MANAGING YOURSELF

CHAPTER 1
FINDING YOUR BALANCE

If you are a first-time, first-line manager, this book is for you. The realities of the manager's job compelled me to write this book, which can be consumed in two ways. The first way is from cover to cover. Doing so will give you access to insights and tools that you can employ to become a balanced and highly effective manager. I encourage you to read this short book in its entirety. The second way to use this book is as a reference that will guide you through complex management challenges. If you have a burning management issue, I invite you to skip to the end of this chapter for the Quick Start Guide. This guide will direct you to the section that covers your issue. This book is about managing yourself and managing your people. There is a lack of material about the fundamentals of management in this context. I've looked, and it's hard to find anything that covers these principles in a "road-tested" practical manner. It's astonishing to me that this void exists. It seems to me that authors want to find some magic formula or one concept that solves all problems. People wrongly assume that managers are born knowing how to manage confrontation, make decisions, create their management persona, hold their people accountable, implement a process for day-to-day management, manage problem people or explosive situations, and fire and hire. These areas form the core of what we cover in this book.

Chapters 2–9 cover areas that were once weaknesses for me. In every instance, I improved through experience, learning things the hard way, listening to my good bosses, taking mental notes from my bad bosses on what not to do, and finally, getting helpful guidance from informal mentors. New and even experienced managers need help from multiple sources. You need someone besides your boss to ask for advice. It can be a relative, a trusted peer, or someone else in another organization. The best mentors have walked in your shoes and share your values. If they've done something similar to what you do, that's even better. When I joined Pepperidge Farm as a district manager, my regional manager asked another district manager, the late Mark Robinson, to "bring me up to speed." He was incredibly helpful and gave me a solid foundation. Nothing can replace the value of a good mentor who is doing or who has done the exact job that you do now. I encourage you to find that person if you can. While not a replacement for a schooled mentor, this book covers areas not specific to any particular job but critical in managing people.

Over my career, I spent seven years as a doer, 11 years as a first-line manager, 14 years as a president, and finally, six years as a CEO of a technology company. I attribute my success to learning how to effectively manage people. My career experience is unusual in that I've never met someone with as much senior leadership experience as I have, who also has 18 years of experience on the front lines. This combination gives me a unique perspective. I've worked for many companies with excellent training programs for individual contributors and then nothing for managers. It's as if these companies believe that merely understanding and excelling at one's job qualifies someone for a management role. Like most managers, I was just "thrown into the fire." We were given a team, and that was it. When we encountered problems, we asked our managers, who had come up the same way, and they offered advice based on their own "trial by fire" experiences. This approach is haphazard at best and is a formula for pain. Pain for the manager and pain for their direct reports. After leaving the corporate world, I opened a coaching practice, reinforcing my belief in the voids I've seen. I've lived the pain, and although you will encounter some pain as you grow in your career, it is my hope that this book can be a resource for you that helps you navigate these challenges more effectively and reduces unnecessary hardships for you and your people.

COMPASSION AND COMMAND

I've titled this book *Compassion And Command* because, in my experience, most new managers lean too much toward one or the other, leading to problems for both the manager and the organization. Where do you fall on the continuum between compassion and command? The mature manager has learned the value of striking a balance between the two and has successfully integrated that approach into their management persona. Let's look at what both overly compassionate and overly commanding managers look like.

The manager whose natural style leans too much toward the compassionate side exhibits many wonderful traits, including empathy, supportiveness, positive reinforcement, open communication, and flexibility, among many others. These are wonderful traits, but I have a saying: "Your strengths are your weaknesses." The meaning of my quote is this: strong traits come with an opposite trait that can often derail a manager's effectiveness. Overly compassionate managers suffer from confrontation avoidance and indecisiveness, can struggle with accountability, can be ineffective in handling problem people, and can struggle with tough decisions. On the other side, commanding managers exhibit focus, confidence, decisiveness, problem-solving skills, and initiative, among many others. However, the other side of the coin is that overly commanding managers can reveal traits that include micromanaging, intimidation tactics, ignoring team feedback, poor communication, and burnout from their people. The best managers I know have developed a leadership persona incorporating positive aspects of compassion and command. Additionally, they have worked to keep the negative traits of their dominant management style to a minimum, resulting in a balanced and highly effective management persona.

COMPASSION And COMMAND

Throughout this book, we cover the fundamentals of management. I've written it with an understanding that the natural style for most new managers is generally either a bit too commanding or compassionate. The chapters in this book blend compassion and command to strike a balance. They will teach you the skills to be highly effective in your manager's role. During my career, I worked for 24 different managers. I would work for 11 of those again. When I look further at the 11, it's easy to say that only three excelled at being compassionate and commanding. They found and lived that balance. I don't know how they started their careers, but I'm sure they were like everyone else. They started in a management role and were either too compassionate or commanding. Over time and through tough lessons, they found balance. They were the best managers that I ever worked for. Working in their organizations has dramatically helped me in my career. To reach your management potential and grow in your career, you must identify your natural style, either compassion or command and actively incorporate elements from that other style to create a balanced management persona. The following story from my early days in management illustrates how managers who are either too compassionate or commanding can experience negative outcomes from their lack of balance.

It was my first job in management, and I was working too hard; I worked six or seven days and over 100 hours most weeks. Looking back, that doesn't even seem possible. My position was out of town in Shelby, NC. I was a district manager with Flowers Foods, a Fortune 500 maker of packaged bakery foods. Most days, I left my home in Charlotte and drove 50 minutes to Shelby. I would need to be at the distribution center by 3:30 AM or 4:00 AM at the latest. I usually arrived home between 7:00 PM and 7:30 PM. One hot summer evening, I fell asleep on I-85.

Fortunately, I awoke with a shot of adrenaline and found myself on the left shoulder just before I headed into the median and into oncoming traffic. I was lucky. I rolled my windows down, turned the music up high, and made it home to my new wife. I had been married for two months. I was not requiring enough from my people and, as a result, needed to work longer and harder to get the job done with nearly disastrous results. I can only imagine the impact my situation almost had on two extended families. I was given a wake-up call and a second chance. I had no guidebook or mentor, so it took me too long, and I experienced too much pain. Eventually, I made the right changes to my overly compassionate management style. I developed a balance between compassionate and commanding management styles. This balanced style has been successful for me and those I've directly managed, those who have managed me, colleagues, and individuals I've mentored in my coaching practice. On the other side, I've worked with multiple overly commanding managers and helped them upskill and add elements from the compassionate side to build a more balanced management persona. Successful managers practice a balanced style.

MANAGING OR LEADING?

Everybody always talks about "leadership," but nobody wants to discuss management and becoming a great manager. My journey from management to leadership taught me a valuable lesson: Effective management lays the groundwork for successful leadership. You cannot ascend to leadership without the foundational respect and trust earned through skilled management. A leader without followers is a failed leader. Through skilled management, one earns the right to lead, guiding one's team beyond the status quo through challenges and toward new opportunities. You must first learn to manage to earn the right to lead people. As I'm sure you know, just because you've got a new title doesn't mean you know anything about managing people. And people won't take direction from you until you demonstrate competence. For this reason, I've chosen to write *Compassion & Command* and be your guide to learning the skills to become a balanced and effective manager.

My Definitions of a Manager and a Leader are as follows:

Manager: "Responsible for administering the current state of affairs." As a district manager at Flowers Foods, I was responsible for retail sales and distribution in Shelby, NC. I was responsible for hiring and firing a distribution center and ensuring that all stores always had fresh bread. I managed the district and all aspects of the people that reported to me.

Leader: "Being responsible for taking a team from the status quo to a new place." Flowers Foods entered the Charlotte market in 1990, and I was on the original team that "broke into" that new market. There were multiple opportunities to lead my team. I led the execution of new initiatives of my own creation and those dictated to me by corporate, but had I not first earned the trust and respect of my teams as a manager, I would never have been able to execute the leadership aspects of the job.

If I could sum up the manager's job in one sentence, it would be this: The manager's job is to manage themselves and others to get the job done. Chapters 2, 3, and 4 in Part 1 of this book focus on managing yourself, your emotions, reactions, and actions. Learning to manage yourself and exercise self-control are valuable and foundational management skills that will serve you well throughout your career. Part 2 applies those newly acquired self-management skills to managing others. *Compassion & Command* is your guide to a balanced approach where effective management meets human understanding. It's designed to help you develop your own unique manager's voice.

QUICK START GUIDE

If you are currently in a burning situation, then I recommend that you first read Chapter 2, 'Conquering Confrontation,' and then skip to the applicable chapter outlined below. Chapter 2 is a prerequisite for the chapters in Part 2, 'Managing Others.' You must conquer confrontation to effectively implement the advice and guidance detailed in Part 2. Use the list below to help you navigate where to go after you read Chapter 2.

- *Hold an employee accountable for something* (**Chapter 5**) If you need to hold an employee responsible for their work or behavior, Chapter 5 details "Managing Individual Performance," an accountability process that you can easily learn and add to your management toolbox.

- *Manage a problem person* (**Chapter 6**) Learn how to identify problem people and the details of the six tools you can employ to manage them.

- *Managing an explosive situation* (**Chapter 7**) Examples of explosive situations and their resolution and details of the six tools you have available to manage explosive situations.

- *Firing an employee* (**Chapter 8**) The details of what to say and how to humanely fire an employee. Including in-person and online video conference termination, Explosive Situation Termination, and layoffs.

- <u>Hiring a new employee</u> (**Chapter 9**) The primary and secondary hiring sources, interview and verification process, red flags, onboarding, and early assessment.

READER TAKEAWAYS

1. **The Compassion and Command Continuum**: Most new managers lean too much toward one or the other. Understand where you are on the continuum.

2. **Balanced Management is the Key to Success**: Adopting a balance between compassion and command through upskilling will lead to lasting success.

3. **Managing Yourself and Others**: The effective manager must manage themselves, their emotions, reactions, and actions actively and deliberately to effectively manage others.

4. **The Quick Start Guide**: If you have a burning situation, reference the quick start guide in this chapter to find helpful solutions to most situations.

CHAPTER EXERCISE

Where Are You on the Compassion to Command Continuum:

- Write down the qualities characterizing your current management style. Are you more compassionate, valuing empathy and approachability, or more commanding, with a focus on decisiveness and driving results? If you need help deciding, ask a few people you trust and who know you well.

- Why do you think you lean toward Compassion or Command? What events in your life led to your current style?

- What qualities from the opposite characteristic do you see value in? Write a list and consider changes to help you become a more balanced manager.

A FINAL THOUGHT

This book provides the tools and insights needed to grow into a balanced and highly effective manager, regardless of your starting point. As I pointed out earlier in the chapter, being too unbalanced in your management style, whether leaning toward being overly compassionate or excessively commanding, can have unforeseen consequences and potentially dangerous results. It's about finding that sweet spot where assertiveness meets empathy. Chapter 2 explores a vital skill for any manager: conquering confrontation.

This journey isn't just about conquering the fear of confrontation but about developing the ability to face challenges confidently and assertively. For the commanding manager, it's an opportunity to refine your approach, ensuring it's impactful yet respectful, balancing firm leadership with open dialogue. Advancing in this area can dramatically propel you toward becoming a manager skilled in navigating a range of people management scenarios, making your management both respected and effective. For the compassionate manager, Chapter 2 offers a path to strengthening assertiveness without sacrificing your natural empathy. It's about enhancing your ability to set clear boundaries and communicate expectations while maintaining your approachability and understanding. This balance will enable you to handle difficult conversations with confidence and resolve, fostering a healthy, productive work environment.

CHAPTER 2
CONQUERING CONFRONTATION

Confrontation is where many new managers find challenges regardless of their initial style. Even skilled and experienced managers can struggle with confrontation. They often must actively remind themselves to act rather than give in to their initial inclination to avoid conflict.

Here is a story from my past that illustrates this point. I was the company president and was 51 years old. I had been in the role for eight years. I knew better. I found myself in a familiar yet challenging situation. Feeling uncertain, I called my brother, who is always a wonderful advisor to me. "Should I fire this person?" I asked, referring to a senior executive that I was close to. He responded, "Of course, you've known you needed to do that for a year." I was floored. I was hiding from confronting this issue. The point here is that leaders and managers at every organizational level struggle with confrontation, and often, you must remind yourself that problems don't disappear.

Managing conflict and confrontation well is essential, and it's important to recognize that this skill is a critical aspect of your role as a manager. The foundational challenge I see is managers struggling to understand the people working for them. They strain to comprehend the motivations that drive people. The big mistake people make is that they start by assuming that people will react and respond to situations similarly to what they would. I see managers fall into the "people are like me" trap. This is officially known as False Consensus Bias. In the management setting, this is where managers believe that their beliefs, values, attitudes, and behaviors exist in the people they manage. This is not true more often than not. In most cases, the people you manage are different.

I've fallen into the "people are like me trap" multiple times. Back when I was a new district manager with Pepperidge Farm. I had a new distributor in a large city in Tennessee. The existing distributors, who I had only recently met, told me they had a warehouse where they received and stored our products (a company requirement). Reluctantly and when pressed, they gave me the address, and I arranged for our brand-new distributor's shipment to be made to this address.

On delivery day, I met my new distributor at the delivery address. The product was delivered, and we had to stack it in the street because there was no warehouse. I had been lied to. I was stunned and shocked that someone would lie to my face, and I didn't know how to react or respond. This was only the beginning of my problems with these distributors. I learned a valuable lesson the hard way: Not everybody you work with has the same values as you do, and you must be prepared for that.

This chapter will explore confrontation, and you will learn a solid, actionable method to integrate respectful confrontation into your management style.

MISMANAGING CONFRONTATION

Throughout the book, we look at ways to help you understand and manage yourself and others. We start by looking at why managers mismanage confrontation. There are two underlying reasons. The first is fear, and the second is simply *not knowing what to do or how to respond*. Fear generally manifests itself in two ways. We look at this from the perspectives of both compassionate and commanding managers.

1. **Compassionate managers often fear:**
    o   hurting their employees' feelings
    o   upsetting their employees
    o   demotivating their employees
    o   making matters worse with the employee
    o   being thought poorly of by their employees, or worse, being disliked.

Science has proven that people overestimate the adverse reactions they will receive from others, known as the Dunning-Kruger effect. The fact is that it is natural and normal to assume that people will be more disturbed and disrupted than they will be. Understanding that does not make initiating a confrontation easier. However, understand that any negative reaction you anticipate is likely worse than what will transpire.

As I write this, I've got a client who recently restructured one of her direct report's areas of responsibility. She just knew this gentleman would not take this well. She was wrong; her direct report said, "Well, if you think that's what's best for the company, then I'm on board." Discussions involving confronting a sensitive subject are not always this easy, but don't blow the repercussions out of proportion in your imagination.

2. **Commanding managers can fear:**
   o **Vulnerability**: There's a concern that showing any sign of emotional openness or uncertainty could be perceived as a weakness. These managers might worry that such vulnerability could undermine their authority or invite challenges to their leadership.
   o **Loss of Control**: This fear is closely tied to the need for order and predictability. Commanding managers might believe that maintaining a strict, commanding presence is essential to keeping things under control. They fear that any deviation from this approach could lead to chaos or diminish their effectiveness as leaders.

Understanding these fears highlights why some managers might lead with an overly commanding style. It's important to realize that strength in leadership is both the ability to be vulnerable and the wisdom to understand that control doesn't only come from authority but also from respect, trust, and collaboration.

By addressing these fears, you can understand that vulnerability is not a liability but a strength that humanizes you and creates connections with your team. Similarly, control can be more effectively maintained through a balanced leadership approach that encourages input and empowers others rather than through intimidation or dominance.

Next, consider all the previously mentioned fears; all these reasons are about you. You are not thinking about the employee and how their lack of performance hurts them and you. You are not thinking about the company either. There is something in your nature that makes you naturally fear this conflict. Many people have this fear, and many have risen above it, mainly through the school of hard knocks. I was on the overly compassionate side and endured too much pain and humiliation in the process of rising above my aversion to confrontation. You can learn from my and others' pain.

The second reason—*not knowing what to do or how to respond to a situation*—is more involved. We partially address that in this chapter and entirely in Part 2 of this book: Managing Others. If you've got a current confrontation need, then after reading this chapter, reference the Quick Start Guide in Chapter 1, which will direct you to where you can likely find help with your specific confrontation.

MASTERING THE CONFRONTATION CONSTRUCT

Effective confrontation management is a hallmark of skilled management, necessitating a delicate balance between compassion and command. The following framework outlines four common pitfalls in confrontation management: Confrontation Avoidance, Spineless Confrontation, Confrontation Without Accountability, and "In Your Face" Confrontation. Addressing these areas builds a management style that's both effective and respected.

CONFRONTATION AVOIDANCE

As we've seen, it's common for managers to avoid the confrontations that management sometimes demands. But here's the kicker: dodging these tough conversations can hold your team back, keeping vital issues in the shadows and hampering growth.

Not all managers are up for the challenge of confronting their team members. I learned this the hard way early in my senior management career. I had a department head under me who couldn't bring himself to confront his team members and have those difficult conversations with his staff. I encouraged him to move forward with the needed confrontations, to no avail. Eventually, I had to move the department head into a different role where he could shine without confronting employees. I brought in someone who could handle those necessary, albeit uncomfortable, conversations. It was a good lesson in the cost of confrontation avoidance for my management journey.

The truth is that seeing confrontation as an opportunity for positive change rather than a storm to be avoided is a mindset shift we all need. If you naturally steer clear of conflict, remember that the fallout from not addressing an issue head-on is almost always worse than biting the bullet and tackling it directly. Think of it this way: "The sooner I face this, the sooner we can move forward." And if you need a rule of thumb, here it is: "The consequences of dodging this issue will always be worse than the discomfort of confronting it."

SPINELESS CONFRONTATION

Here's the thing about spineless confrontation—it's when you kinda, sorta confront someone but not really. It's like saying, "Hey, the big boss isn't thrilled with that red T-shirt under your uniform. Me? I don't really mind, but rules are rules, right?" That's not the way to do it. You've got to own your role and your decisions. You're the boss, and you shouldn't run from your responsibilities.

I learned this firsthand in one of my early management roles. My boss, Steve, was visiting our distribution center and noticed one of my new route salespeople, a "breadman," came back with 12 loaves of unsold bread. Fresh bread in the truck at the end of the day is against policy and is a recipe for high stale and high costs. Steve's solution was to send the breadman back out, and I was the messenger. My delivery? "Steve wants you to go back out with the bread." This was a mistake on so many levels. It positioned Steve as the bad guy implied I was indifferent to our policies, and showed me as a pushover.

If I could do it over, I'd have a candid talk with Steve about the decision and ask for an exception due to the newness of the employee, then explain to my breadman the reasons behind our no-truck stock policy, making it clear that future infractions would mean heading back out to distribute any unsold bread.

Hiding behind phrases like "the boss is unhappy" or "it's just policy" doesn't cut it. You must be direct, take ownership, explain the policy, and show empathy. If the thought of confrontation makes you uneasy, you're not alone. It feels awkward, especially at first, but it does get easier with time. And it's crucial. It clarifies your stance to the team, and even more critically, it clarifies their standing. It demonstrates that you're not just a figurehead but a manager with the courage to make tough calls and the empathy to understand your team.

CONFRONTATION WITHOUT ACCOUNTABILITY

Let's not mince words: accountability is the backbone of effective confrontation, but without it, even the most skillfully navigated confrontations can fail to achieve results. It's one thing to address an issue head-on but another to follow through and ensure real change or improvement. As managers, it's our job to set clear expectations right from the get-go and to lay out the consequences if these aren't met.

This isn't about swinging the hammer every chance you get. It's about striking the right balance between being firm on standards and fair, considering the unique circumstances each time. It means coming up with solutions that are not just about keeping the wheels turning but about moving forward constructively for everyone involved.

Effective confrontation involves initial interaction with your employee and then following up. You must follow up to create accountability. We deeply dive into making accountability a seamless part of your confrontation strategy in Chapter 5. It's packed with methods for effective follow-up after every confrontation, ensuring that every discussion leads to tangible outcomes.

"IN YOUR FACE" CONFRONTATION

This confrontational style is seen in managers who go all out with their commanding style, always choosing directness and aiming for quick results, sometimes at the expense of careful communication and team harmony. Yes, demonstrating command is a key part of management. Still, when it turns into aggression, it can start chipping away at the trust and respect you've worked so hard to build.

The real challenge for those with a natural "in your face" approach is to dial down the intensity without losing the impact. It's about threading compassion into your commanding style, ensuring that even the tough conversations are handled with professionalism, focusing squarely on the problem, and treating each individual with respect. Getting this balance right can transform the workplace, turning confrontations into opportunities for growth and strengthening the team.

From what I've seen, managers who lead with this high-octane style often end up being viewed negatively by their team. They're either feared, resented, or both, which can lead to high turnover—something I've witnessed more times than I'd like to remember.

If you recognize yourself in this description, take heart. Your commanding style is a powerful tool. By softening your approach a bit, you can turn it into a force for good that inspires loyalty rather than fear. It's about showing your team you're firm, fair, and understanding. This shift can make all the difference, enhancing your management and making your team more cohesive and committed.

INTEGRATING BALANCED CONFRONTATION

By understanding and adjusting these confrontation styles, managers can develop a balanced approach that leverages the strengths of both compassion and command. This balanced approach is critical to resolving issues efficiently while maintaining and building positive team dynamics. As you become adept at navigating confrontations with a mix of command and compassion, you set the stage for a thriving, respectful, and high-performing team.

HOW TO CONFRONT YOUR PEOPLE

As a manager, it is your job to keep your company's and your people's best interests at the forefront of your mind. This is a balancing act. There is one relationship that you need to manage here. You must control the relationship between your people and your company and be "*Fair to the company and fair to the employee.*" This one simple concept should be your North Star and will go a long way toward helping you settle and solve issues.

FAIR TO THE COMPANY AND FAIR TO THE EMPLOYEE

This may seem obvious, but in my experience, this simple principle is lost on most people. Things go wrong if you go all in toward the company or the employee. The most common thing I see is managers worrying only about their people and always siding with them. That is an example of avoiding confrontation and taking the path of least resistance or the easy way out. Over the years, I've had multiple sales managers come to me and explain that two salespeople worked on a particular deal, and they would like me to pay both of them full commission on the deal. In special cases, this may be appropriate. For the manager, double commission is a great solution. The manager is free from conflict, and both salespeople are delighted. But is that fair to the company? No, not in most cases. The answer is to look at multiple ways to divide the commission and potentially examine paying more. I would not rush to double the commission because a simple commission split may be fine. An unending number of situations can be better dealt with if the manager refers back to the simple principle of always looking at the problem from the joint perspective of the company and the employee. The employee is great at hitting the manager with the employee's perspective, and the manager gets showered with requests in favor of the employee all day long. I would have managers come to me with a "situation," and I would simply explain that their job was to be fair to the company and fair to the employees. Once I explained that to them, they were visibly relieved. Less experienced managers tend to think that things will fall either on the side of the company or the employee, and they come to me with a situation, advocating for the employee. Once they understand that it rarely must be all in favor of the employee or the company, they relax and begin to bring me creative solutions that satisfy both parties.

Most employees will understand that it can't all be one way.

THE CONFRONTATION PROCESS

When preparing for a confrontation, it's important to remember the Dunning-Kruger effect, which states that people tend to overestimate the negative outcomes of difficult conversations. Use the following three-step process to guide you:

1. **Prepare and Rehearse**: Plan your conversation carefully and rehearse your words. Ensure your approach is fair to both the company and the employee. Anticipate the possible positive, negative, or neutral reactions and be ready to respond appropriately.

2. **Stay Focused**: Be direct and avoid diluting your message with unrelated compliments or positives. Mixing the issue with unrelated praise can confuse the employee. Keep the conversation focused on the problem and conclude the meeting by expressing appreciation for their willingness to address the issue.

3. **Follow-Up**: Mark your calendar to follow up on the situation as needed. If you suspect the confrontation may not go well, consider reading Chapter 6 on Managing Problem People. This chapter offers concise guidance

to help you confidently navigate more challenging confrontations.

If this is the first time you've had a real conversation with this person in three months, that needs to change. We cover that in Chapter 5, where I show you a simple process for regularly checking in with and managing your people.

It's essential to ensure that your interactions with your team aren't limited to confrontations; meaningful business conversations should occur regularly.

CONFRONTATION AND THE THREE PROBLEM TYPES

A great mantra for you to live by is: "Problems don't go away; they get worse over time." If you live by this mantra and confront problems with appropriate action, you will be ahead of most managers with whom I've crossed paths. I want to qualify that statement; from what I've seen, some problems do "go away," and that problem type is always the same. I've seen many "problem" employees resign before the supervisor addressed the issue. You are far better off addressing and managing the issue on your terms rather than just waiting and hoping things will work out independently. Here are the three types of problems:

1. Problems you know and acknowledge.

2. Problems you suspect but are afraid or reluctant to pull back the covers on.
3. Problems you are unaware of.

PROBLEMS YOU KNOW AND ACKNOWLEDGE

These are problems that you know and acknowledge yet haven't addressed. You've just learned the three-step process of how to confront an employee and manage a situation. Work the plan. Congratulations in advance for taking action.

PROBLEMS YOU SUSPECT BUT ARE AFRAID OR RELUCTANT TO PULL BACK THE COVERS ON

You suspect something's wrong; you've just got a "feeling" or overheard something. You don't know for sure, so you choose to ignore it. In my experience, there is a problem, and problems get worse over time, so it is always better to look into things when something doesn't feel right. Waiting is always a bad idea. I've also experienced the negative consequences of confrontation avoidance.

Here is an example from my days as a CEO. I watched as our VP of sales continued to look the other way when one of her salespeople would "steal" other salespeople's deals. Our salespeople grew tired of complaining to her because she failed to fix the problem, and they began bringing this to my attention. I met with her on multiple occasions, and she assured me that she had met with the offending salesperson and that things were all straightened out. She said it was all just a misunderstanding. I expected my managers to "run" their operations and gave them the latitude to do so. An intervention by me was the exception, not the rule. The problem persisted for six months. One day, my VP of sales came to me and told me that we needed to fire this "deal-stealing" salesperson. She had uncovered an array of unethical behaviors that this salesperson was engaged in, including having a separate business where he improperly sold our data and information to his customers. Not only was he stealing deals from his peers on our sales team, but he was also directly stealing money from our company. We looked further and found more misdeeds.

As we've seen, many of us have natural aversions to dealing with conflict. As I stated already, you are always better off proactively managing this. If you hear something that doesn't sound right, look into it. You will get better at this over time, and you will come to take pride and satisfaction in doing your job well. You will go from a place of fear and trepidation to one of pride and confidence. I've often seen the positive impacts of proactive confrontation in my junior managers and clients.

PROBLEMS YOU ARE UNAWARE OF

I know a CEO who used to tell people that his job was "to try and not be the last one to know." Managers are always the last to know. I hate this reality. The reality is that things are going on in your organization that need to be addressed by you, but you are unaware of them. When the CEO I mentioned took over his most recent role, he met with his new employees and held small round-table discussions. He asked: "What should I know now that I'm going to find out anyway?" People opened up, and he moved the business forward much faster. Hidden problems are a tricky category to manage. Still, you need to realize that there are always things the manager does not know about. Keep your ears and eyes open and look into rather than away from things.

ADOPTING A BALANCED CONFRONTATION STYLE

I've observed various management styles, from overly confrontational or commanding to exceedingly compassionate. Each style has its unique challenges. Today's workplace environment often rejects harsh or overbearing management, leading to high staff turnover and dissatisfaction under overly commanding managers. Conversely, excessively compassionate managers may find enforcing rules and making tough decisions challenging, potentially impacting team effectiveness and growth. Fortunately, each style harbors the seeds of balanced, effective management. Take what you've learned in this chapter to develop your balanced style.

CONFRONTING CUSTOMER ISSUES

This book is not about managing customers, but many managers face customer confrontation. I wanted to include this brief section with some helpful insights.

The critical thing to keep in mind is the need to start the process of dealing with a customer situation immediately. I used to get complaints from grocery store managers on my voicemail. "I've not seen my cookie man in months." I doubted it had been months, but I needed the facts. My territory consisted of three states, and some of my stores could be a five-hour drive from my home office, so making an in-person visit was not always a good option. I learned that in every instance, the sooner I could make phone contact with the complaining party, the better. This held true when I was a District Manager with Pepperidge Farm and the CEO of a technology company. The formula is the same. Get the customer on the phone as soon as possible, listen to all they have to say, and then thank them. Tell them that you need to dig into the situation and will get back to them. Respond as the situation dictates. I can't think of a situation where the complaining party didn't give me time to investigate and resolve the situation. In every situation, the manager or complaining party was relieved and calmed down after my one interaction with them. That one phone call had made an enormous difference. Now, you have to resolve things, but the sooner you can respond, the better, and that is ALWAYS true. We have a natural human tendency to avoid pain, but waiting will cause more pain. The same is true with all the issues you face. The sooner you start working on them, the better.

Final note: I encourage you to avoid taking the easy way out by communicating with a complaining party on an electronic platform. I'm not going to get into everything that can go wrong here. Still, electronic platforms can sometimes further escalate an already negative situation. CALL YOUR CUSTOMER; if you don't get them, leave them a voicemail asking for a return call. Some customers will never be happy, and there will be the occasional customer who wants to ruin your day, but MOST people are reasonable.

READER TAKEAWAYS

- Confrontation is a key part of your job, and you should know that and actively take steps to address and confront issues early and resolve them promptly.

- Confrontation is uncomfortable for most people I've managed, coached, and worked with. People, including you and me, will do almost anything to avoid awkward situations.

- You must master confrontation to become an effective manager.

- A straightforward and candid approach is always best when dealing with a problematic issue. Trying to sandwich a negative between two positives usually confuses people, and you likely won't achieve the desired result. Put time on your calendar for a follow-up.

- Most people overestimate the negative consequences and reactions they will get by being open and candid with people about difficult topics. Don't assume your employee or customer will negatively react to your topic.

- Learning to effectively confront people, practicing that skill, and getting good at it will change your career trajectory.

CHAPTER EXERCISE

1. **Identify a Specific Challenge**: Think of a specific confrontation you need to have. It could be anything from addressing a team member's performance issue to discussing a repeated delay in project deadlines.

2. **Apply the Three-Step Process**:

   - **Prepare and Rehearse**: Plan your conversation carefully and rehearse your words. Ensure your approach is fair to both the company and the employee. Anticipate the possible positive, negative, or neutral reactions and be ready to respond appropriately.
   - **Conduct the Meeting**: Be direct and avoid diluting your message with unrelated compliments or positives. Mixing the issue with unrelated praise can confuse the employee. Keep the conversation focused on the problem and conclude the meeting by

expressing appreciation for their willingness to address the issue.

- **Follow-Up**: Mark your calendar to follow up on the situation as needed. If you suspect the confrontation may not go well, consider reading Chapter 6 on Managing Problem People.

3. **Role-Playing (Optional)**: Role-play this confrontation with a trusted colleague or mentor if possible. I know this can sound "hokey," but I've been involved in role-playing throughout my career, and it's valuable. This can help you refine your approach and build confidence.

- **Reflect and Analyze**: After executing your plan, reflect on how it went. What worked well? What could be improved? Did the outcome align with your goals?

Note: Remember, this exercise aims to help you grow as a manager. Confrontation is a skill that improves with practice, so don't worry if it's not perfect the first time. The important thing is to take that first step and learn from the experience.

A Final Thought

When I look back to the example earlier in this chapter, I had to face the fact that I needed to terminate someone I had a close relationship with. I had 17 years of experience managing people at that point in my career. I had been the company president for eight years. Yet, even with all this experience, I still struggled with confronting a personnel issue. I had known the individual in question for a long time and had a personal relationship with him. I had been a pallbearer at his father's funeral. Nonetheless, over lunch, I did what I needed to do. On the five-minute ride back to the office, he was relieved and discussed what he would do next. The next day, he came into the office and told me he had been unhappy for a long time and that he was relieved that his job was over and excited about new beginnings. My senior constituents were impressed with how well I handled this, and things moved forward positively. I'm proud of how I handled it and am still friends with this former employee today. That said, you can't count on difficult terminations always going this well, but realize that confronting issues head-on is a skill you will improve over time, and tackling issues earlier is always better than delaying the inevitable. Learning why you avoid confrontation, the problems it causes, and how to properly manage it are tremendous skills and prerequisites for sound decision-making.

It's time to move on to a huge issue I once was terrible at: making timely decisions. In the next chapter, we learn to become great at making sound and timely decisions.

CHAPTER 3
DECISION-MAKING

Midway through my 14-year tenure as President of EDA, our corporate executive team initiated a 360-review process. In these 360 reviews, individuals are evaluated by their superiors, peers, and subordinates. I only remember one thing about that process: my lowest score was in decision-making. When I look back on that time, I can see why. I struggled with decisions on multiple fronts. I was slow to make decisions, and when you're in management, others are waiting on your answers so they can do their jobs. I also tended to avoid addressing difficult situations. This problem was a blend of confrontation avoidance and decision-making paralysis. The low score bothered me, so I made a concerted effort to improve.

YOUR DECISION-MAKING STYLE

Just as in managing confrontation, your approach to decision-making can also lean toward either compassion or command. Compassionate decision-makers often prioritize the well-being and input of their team, sometimes at the cost of speed and decisiveness. Commanding decision-makers, on the other hand, may prioritize efficiency and clarity but risk overlooking their decisions' emotional and relational impacts. Recognizing where you fall on this spectrum allows you to adjust your approach, integrating both styles to make balanced, effective decisions.

FOUR REASONS WHY PEOPLE STRUGGLE WITH DECISIONS

Eventually, I became good at making decisions, but not until I developed a formal process to help me. Subsequently, I noticed that many managers in my organization struggled with decision-making. I shared my process and actively worked to assist them, making me more effective in my role. I'll walk you through the decision-making process later in this chapter in the "Decision and Execution Framework" section. Still, first, we must address the root causes of decision avoidance. If you don't struggle with decisions, great. But if you do, it's essential to understand why. I see four main reasons why people struggle with decisions:

1. Fear of Confrontation
2. Fear of Making a Mistake
3. Confusing the Making of a Decision with the Execution of That Decision
4. Not Knowing What to Do

Sometimes, these reasons overlap. The good news is that you will grow and improve with practice. I subscribe to the philosophy that "speed is better than perfection." That means you will make mistakes, and depending on your role, the number of decisions you need to make could be huge. It is estimated that sales managers in the SaaS (Software as a Service) business, an industry I worked in for 20 years, make dozens of decisions daily. Multiply two dozen decisions by the number of working days, and you get close to 6,000 decisions annually. During my time in SaaS, I easily made thousands of decisions yearly. The best principle I've found is "speed over perfection." We can all handle the "no-brainers;" the difficult decisions trip us up and slow down our entire organization. If you struggle with any of the items on the list above, you can easily get paralyzed. Know that you can learn to become a great decision-maker.

Fear of Confrontation

Chapter 2 has given you the tools to move past this. The decision-making arena is precisely where you can begin to practice and perfect your developing skills in effective confrontation. I encourage you to get started. But if you struggle to make decisions, keep reading.

Fear of Making a Mistake

The fear of making a mistake is a common problem that significantly obstructs decision-making, especially in management roles. It involves the anxiety and apprehension of the possibility of making wrong decisions and facing their consequences. Moving past this fear involves acknowledging its presence, understanding its sources, and developing strategies to manage it effectively.

I've had multiple managers who worked for me and were terrified of making a mistake. They never wanted to be wrong; they wanted to be perfect. I tended to see this trait in managers who had a commanding style. They felt like they would lose their credibility and control if they made any mistakes. If you struggle with that, you need to get past it and understand that managers who admit mistakes are stronger and more effective than those who hide behind the veil of perfection.

I want to be right. Everybody wants to be right. When I took over a troubled acquisition, it was my first time in a senior management role. I was now making broader decisions, like choosing our healthcare provider and what benefits we would offer our people. My parent company constantly pushed me to combine my healthcare plan with theirs. After six years of contracting with different providers, I decided to go with what corporate wanted. They would administer the plan, which would exactly mirror our benefits. At the time, there were roughly 75 people in my organization. I was concerned but felt things would go well.

The healthcare transition was a disaster. It ruined my year. We had phenomenal business results that year—maybe the best in my entire career—but that will be forever overshadowed by the disastrous healthcare switch. The head of my HR department told me that we had people who needed medical care but were avoiding the doctor because they feared they wouldn't be covered. That's like having no insurance. It took a year to resolve this, and we eventually went back to a separate plan. This scenario reinforced my slow and measured approach to decision-making. It further carried me down the wrong road. As I mentioned, it was only after my poor scores on decision-making in my 360 review that I realized I had a real problem with making timely decisions.

Making timely and sound decisions is a skill you can practice, learn, and get good at. I have had several managers who reported to me who couldn't make decisions without first running them by me in great detail. They shared a similar characteristic: a massive fear of making mistakes and an almost unwillingness to admit they were wrong. So they would do all the work, study a situation, and come to me with a lot of research and completed homework. They would know exactly what needed to be done. But the fear of being wrong paralyzed them and kept them from moving forward. Ultimately, they wanted me to make the decision. So, in the end, it was my decision, and if it was wrong, I would be on the hook. That was fine with me, except that I now had to dive into an unusually complex situation that might involve evaluating multiple vendors or many interviews. It was a time crush for me.

The inability to make decisions will negatively impact your career, as illustrated by this story from my father. I have vivid memories of my father, a commander in the Navy when I was a senior in high school. He was frustrated one evening and spoke to me about his second in command, Bob Johnson, a lieutenant commander who had been passed over for promotion to the rank of commander several times. Dad said, "Bob is great, and many 'flowery things' have been written about him in his fitness reports over the years. Still, Bob's fitness reports omit a critical flaw in his management acumen; they don't say he cannot make decisions. Bob cannot make decisions."

I didn't appreciate what that meant then, but decades later, I remembered that exchange with Dad and came to understand and appreciate his frustration. Over the years, I could coach many of my managers past this, but I did have a few that I could never coach past it. Again, if you can't get past the fear of making decisions, I suggest finding someone to coach or counsel you. Conquering this one area will do wonders for your career.

Confusing Making a Decision with the Execution of That Decision

Making a decision and executing a decision are two different sides of the same coin. I've seen with my clients and experienced in my career that leaders tend to confuse the decision with the execution.

Take my example at the beginning of Chapter 2. I had a problematic termination looming, and my mind jumped to my fear of confronting and firing this individual. As a result, I didn't decide for nearly a year. I was consumed with worries about executing what I thought needed to happen. As soon as I addressed it and made the decision, it was over in 10 days. When you have a difficult situation, be sure to separate the decision from the execution in your mind.

Use the decision-making process in this chapter to help you decide, and then use the confrontation process in Chapter 2 to aid with the confrontation.

Not Knowing What to Do

Not knowing how to solve the problem or what the best solution is out of a series of possibilities is a difficult position to be in. You have a situation and have no idea how to solve it. Amazingly, you will never see everything and never stop encountering new situations throughout your career. This sounds daunting, but the good news is that after you gain experience, you will realize that although every problem is different, situations tend to fit into broad categories. You will be able to handle them similarly. The best thing I've found to help with the decision-making process when I didn't know what to do is the 'Decision and Execution Framework' that I discovered somewhere and then tweaked and built out over the years. Read on as we dig into that.

DECISION AND EXECUTION FRAMEWORK

Use this astonishingly simple and straightforward framework for every decision you don't know how to solve.

THE FRAMEWORK

Date:

Problem Situation/Current Status: Describe the problem or situation and its current status in one sentence. A well-defined problem is half-solved.

List Your Alternatives: Write down your ideas, ask others for suggestions, and consider whether there is a better alternative. There are always two solutions to a problem: 1) the obvious answer and 2) doing nothing. Always search for the third option and maybe a fourth. Never have more than four options, as the brain gets overwhelmed after four. Most people only consider the first two.

Decide: The word "decision" comes from the Latin word "decisio," meaning "to cut off." Consider and compare the pros and cons of each alternative, get buy-in, and then decide on the alternative that best solves your problem.

Execution: List the actions to be taken by whom and when.

That's it. It is an astonishingly simple process. I've found it to be very effective.

THE POWER OF DECISION-MAKING

Over the years, I became quite good at making speedy decisions. Taking initiative and making decisions had much to do with my career success. But the higher I rose, the more challenging the decisions became. Many of the decisions I had to make were brought to me by talented managers who came to me only after they had spent a good deal of time trying to decide for themselves; as you can imagine, these could be challenging. In the end, I discovered that routine decisions far outnumbered the difficult ones. I found myself making a large number of routine or relatively easy choices. However, I kept the "Decision and Execution Framework" on a sheet of paper in my desk drawer. I used it about once every six months to help me move when I was stuck in a situation. I was always surprised by how effective this simple process was in helping me move forward.

You need to get good at making timely decisions. You always want to be correct, but you should prioritize decision speed over always being right. You will improve over time; your senior management will respect you for taking the initiative and keeping things moving. You will get more responsibility. Depending on the problem or situation, it could take months to resolve, so it's essential to keep things moving and address multiple concerns simultaneously. If I handled only one problem at a time, I tended to fixate on it, which caused me stress. This sounds strange, but I relaxed and was less stressed when addressing multiple problems simultaneously. Maybe I felt good because a plan was in place and progress was being made on numerous fronts, or maybe it was because various situations kept me from focusing too much on any one problem. Either way, addressing multiple situations helped my peace of mind.

DEALING WITH WRONG DECISIONS

When you make a bad decision, here's what to do:

1. **Take Total Ownership**: Own the decision completely. This responsibility helps calm all parties involved and maintains your credibility as the manager.

2. **Take Corrective Action**: Act swiftly to correct and fix the issues your decision caused. Addressing problems head-on is crucial for minimizing negative impacts.

3. **Move On**: After resolving the issue, move forward. Focus on your next decision and apply the lessons you've learned. Every mistake is an opportunity to improve your decision-making skills.

4. **Learn and Improve**: Understand that it's impossible to get everything right. Embrace

the learning process and know that each experience makes you better at handling future challenges.

I can't overstate the importance of getting great at consistently making timely decisions. It shows confidence. Learn to be totally fine with a certain level of wrong choices in favor of moving forward on all the great things associated with the speedy decisions you made that were right on target. Follow the process of the decision framework; decide and move on. Your people, organization, and career will be better for it.

READER TAKEAWAYS

- Not making sound and timely decisions will negatively impact your team, organization, and career.

- Prioritize decision speed over always being right.

- If you struggle to make decisions, it's likely because of one of four reasons:

  - Fear of Confrontation

  - Fear of Making a Mistake

  - Confusing the Making of a Decision with the Execution of That Decision

  - Not Knowing What to Do

- Use the Decision and Execution Framework to jumpstart your process and make timely decisions.

CHAPTER EXERCISE

1. **Identify Your Decision-Making Challenges**: Reflect on the four reasons people struggle with decisions discussed earlier in this chapter. Identify which of these reasons often holds you back from making timely decisions.

2. **List Your Current Decisions**: Make a list of decisions you must make. Order them by priority, focusing on those that impact your team's performance and your effectiveness as a manager.

3. **Apply the Decision and Execution Framework**: For each decision on your list, use the Decision and Execution Framework to break down the process. Be sure to consult with others on possible solutions. Write down the problem, generate alternatives, weigh the pros and cons, and decide on the best action. Take action.

4. **Reflect on Outcomes**: Reflect on the outcomes after making and implementing your decisions. What worked well? What could have been done differently? Use these

insights to refine your decision-making process going forward.

A Final Thought

As you head down the road of making well-thought-out and timely decisions, you will begin to feel empowered and emboldened. Your self-confidence will also rise, and your team's performance will improve. But there are a few more ingredients that a team needs to succeed. Keep reading as we explore this further in "Creating Your Management Persona."

CHAPTER 4
CREATING YOUR
MANAGEMENT PERSONA

I've saved the actual creation of your management persona for the exercise at the end of the chapter. While reading, pay attention to areas that resonate with you, knowing that you will build them into your management persona.

Your management persona is who you are as a manager. It's the person everyone at your company sees. It's how you behave, handle things, and relate to people in the work environment. People are many things: parents, children, workers, spouses, coaches, community members, and managers. All of these are different personas, and just as you actively decide the characteristics you exhibit as a parent, you should also actively decide on and demonstrate the characteristics that define your management style. Don't leave this to chance.

The following story illustrates how I effectively used a personal experience to help cement one of the four management persona building blocks, "Create Hope and Certainty," at EDA after being introduced as their new president.

I was driving a rental car in midtown Manhattan. It was a beautiful morning, but it was September 11, 2001. To my knowledge, I was never in any danger, but I did witness both towers burning. I stayed in New

York and the surrounding area that entire week. In retrospect, I should have just driven the 1000-plus miles home because although nearly all my meetings were still conducted, they were not productive. It was an emotional place to be in the direct aftermath of the attacks. I drove home on Friday and Saturday. It took almost 20 hours. Ironically, on Monday, when I returned to corporate, I was promoted to the president of a troubled acquisition, EDA, that we had acquired two years prior.

Like nearly everyone everywhere in the United States, my new team was worried and preoccupied about the events of 9/11. One of the things I addressed at my first companywide meeting was the new state of the world and how America had lived through many times that were much worse than 9/11. I cited several examples, including WWII and the Civil War. I grew to understand that to be effective in my new role, I needed to create hope and certainty, take charge, earn respect through my actions, and be authentically me.

You need to develop and integrate four building blocks into your management persona. To effectively manage, your people need you to:

1. Create Hope and Certainty

2. Take Charge

3. Be Admired and Respected

4. Be Yourself

THE BUILDING BLOCKS

1. CREATE HOPE AND CERTAINTY

Basic human needs are hope, certainty, and the need to feel safe. Your people look to you to satisfy these needs. Compassionate managers often excel in providing emotional support and reassurance, creating a sense of security through their understanding and empathy. However, they may need to incorporate more command by being decisive and clear about expectations, ensuring their team feels secure through empathy and leadership. Conversely, managers with a commanding style might be excellent at setting clear directions and providing stability through decisiveness. Still, they may need to soften their approach to consider the emotional impact on their team.

I faced multiple changes in company ownership, the 9/11 crisis, the dot-com bubble burst, the Great Recession, and COVID-19. These were just the big headline-grabbing issues; we had multiple challenges at corporate and within the businesses I ran over that same time frame, and this is normal. People's need for certainty never ends, and being responsible for calming the troops can get exhausting. But it's the manager's job. Embrace it and remember that all people are primarily interested in themselves, so they worry about how change affects them. The underlying root cause of all their fears is uncertainty. People just don't know what's around the corner, and of course, some people are less adept at handling uncertainty than others. Make no mistake; no one likes too much uncertainty, including you. You are in a management role, and you may look forward to the ability to craft the future, but what if you heard that your boss was leaving? That would change things for you. You must be prepared to deal with the never-ending uncertainty in your business and the world.

I addressed our teams at two companies almost every Monday morning for 20 years. This included navigating through all of those world-changing events I just mentioned. There were many times when I didn't want to face my people for one reason or another. But they required me to be the manager they needed. I pushed through my occasional anxiety and self-doubt, trying my best to be what I often advise people to be when facing uncertainty: "An Iron Stake Hammered into a Frozen Ground." When you run into things you don't have an answer for, your response should always be the same: "I don't know, but we will figure it out; we always have," or something similar. It doesn't matter what the situation is; you always need to respond similarly: "I know this doesn't look good right now" or "Wow, this is unfortunate, but it will be fine, and we as a team will figure it out—we always have, right?" When you think about it, what's the alternative? To shut down operations and close? No. Be the iron stake; be the hope and certainty your team needs.

Depending on your natural disposition, this may take work. Compassionate managers may need to work on confidently asserting that things will be okay while commanding managers might need to show they understand the emotional strain on their team.

Still, I assure you that your team and company need this, which will pay dividends for your career. I was on the overly compassionate side of the spectrum and became the "Iron stake hammered into a frozen ground" regarding hope and certainty—and you can, too.

2. TAKE CHARGE

Your company put you in charge; your people need that from you. Compassionate managers often struggle with taking charge because they are concerned about being liked or upsetting the team. They need to learn that taking command does not mean being unkind—it means being decisive for the good of the team. On the other hand, commanding managers might find it easy to take charge. Still, they should be mindful of how their decisions impact team morale. It's about finding the right balance.

You have been put in charge and should take charge and run with it. My daughter-in-law works for Nike; Nike would say: "Just Do It." The more you take total ownership of your management role, the better. I was overwhelmed with a task when I was 31 years old and an inexperienced district manager. My boss met with me and explained that he could do the particular item I was struggling with, but in the end, he said, "Now, if I do this, then I'm doing your job, and if I'm doing your job, what do I need you for?" I didn't appreciate that comment, but he was right. It took me too long, but I finally began owning my responsibility. Once I did, I enjoyed being in charge, making decisions, having successes, and fixing my mistakes. It was empowering and emboldened me.

I was a new senior manager at a different company many years later. Remembering that the first charge of a new manager is to learn and observe, I attended the management team meeting, and my predecessor, my new second-in-command, ran it as usual. He came to a point in the meeting where he reviewed a situation with a few alternate solutions, and I watched as he held a vote. He went with the solution that got the most votes. I was amazed. This is wrong on every level. For starters, you and only you are responsible for your team and the results. Would you really abdicate your responsibility for decision-making? Some people refer to that kind of process as the democratic process. That's not how a democracy works. People vote for the president, but once president, the commander-in-chief is in charge and wields that power.

If you reference the "Decision-Making" chapter, you will notice I'm all for getting input. I bet I went with my people's recommendations over 90% of the time, but I never held a vote, and you shouldn't either. You will never be an effective manager if you don't consistently get input and buy-in from your team, but you are in charge and need to own the decisions. You must acknowledge your role and responsibility, take charge, make decisions, and move forward. This is in the best interest of the company, your people, and your career. As you practice this, you will get better and more comfortable with it over time. If management is genuinely for you, I expect you will come to enjoy and take pride in running your own show.

3. BE ADMIRED AND RESPECTED

People want to admire and respect the manager they work for. Respect and admiration often stem from a blend of compassion and command. Compassionate managers gain respect through their understanding and support. But also must demonstrate command by holding people accountable. Commanding managers may be admired for their decisiveness, but they should incorporate compassion to build stronger, more genuine connections with their teams.

Astonishingly, during my career, I had three bosses who had extramarital affairs with people who worked for them. I subsequently learned about two affairs after those bosses were no longer with the organization. However, in the third instance, I discovered the situation while reporting to this boss. I lost respect for them, a feeling that persisted for years, and although I never broached the topic, the boss's halo was gone. People are human, and I get that, but I have always wanted to work for the best. I wanted my boss or manager to be great—the best manager to ever command a team.

The good news about your role is that people want to admire and respect the manager they work for all day and all year. They want you to have unique qualities and be of good character. People spend most of their adult lives working and want those years to mean something. They want to feel like they are working for someone they admire and respect. You can and should be that person.

As a bread route district manager, I was one of four district managers out of the Charlotte distribution center. Carl was a fellow manager. His personal life was a mess. He was always leaving the distribution center during work hours to bail someone out of jail, help someone after a car accident, or take someone to the hospital after a drug overdose. I've never experienced anything like it. I've seen people with problems, but I don't remember working with anyone in management whose life was always in such an uproar. One day, one of his people approached me and said, "Carl's a good guy, but he's got too many personal problems to be a manager. We need someone who is here and who can help us." Carl was a good guy, and I liked him, but something was off about his personal life. That's an extreme case, but the point is that your people want to think you are smart, capable, of high integrity, and a role model. This list goes on and on. Carl's people didn't appreciate that he always had to leave for some personal crisis. People have outsized expectations for their manager. The more you can walk the walk and be someone they respect and admire, the more respect and admiration you will garner.

We are human, and no one should expect perfection from a manager. I'm not advocating that you aspire to perfection. But I encourage you to be the manager you would want to work for. Compassionate managers should ensure they're respected not just for their kindness but also for their ability to make tough calls. Commanding managers should aim to be admired not just for their decisiveness but also for their empathy. People don't like to work for those they don't respect, so balancing compassion and command is essential for earning admiration and respect.

4. BE YOURSELF

I saved this section for last because it's the most challenging. It was for me. It will be a challenge for you because you need to "be yourself" in the context of a management role and in the context of the previous three sections in this chapter: "Creating Hope and Certainty," "Taking Charge," and being someone who is "Admired and Respected."

Maybe you have work to do crafting your management persona to effectively incorporate those three elements. As you work toward building "yourself" into your management persona, remember that you're unique and want that uniqueness to become part of your persona. Whether you are an introvert, an extrovert, or somewhere in between, you bring yourself and all your uniqueness to the table. Understanding where you naturally lean toward compassion or command will help you create a more balanced and authentic management persona. If you tend to be more compassionate, embrace that quality, but also work on asserting yourself when needed. If you're naturally commanding, continue managing with authority, but remember to integrate empathy and understanding into your interactions.

I have a great client named Abby. While working with her, I've told her multiple times, "I want you to be Abby. I don't ever want you to not be Abby; you've got wonderful natural characteristics." I work with Abby to help bring some of her less-developed talents to the surface. She is naturally a very altruistic person. She deeply cares about her people and genuinely wants the best for them. They see that, and the result is an amazing amount of loyalty. She's got their back, and they would do anything for her. The point here is that you've got great qualities that are the backbone of who you are. You should incorporate them into your management persona.

Your charge is to create hope and certainty, take charge, and do so in a way that people will admire and respect—all over a backdrop of bringing a personal style and flair that ONLY you can bring to that role. Being yourself in your management role doesn't mean staying within your comfort zone; it means understanding your strengths and working to incorporate elements from both compassion and command to become a more balanced and effective leader.

READER TAKEAWAYS

1. Your people always need hope and certainty; always create that for them.

2. You've been given command by your company, so take charge; everyone needs you to.

3. People want to admire and respect their manager; be the manager you would want to work for.

4. It's critical to authentically be yourself. Work to incorporate elements of your personality into your management persona.

CHAPTER EXERCISE

- **Getting specific about who you are**: Write down your unique characteristics. Are you an introvert, an extrovert, or somewhere in between? Are you more inclined to lead with compassion, or do you find yourself taking a more commanding stance? Consider your sense of humor, interests, and personal qualities.

- **Create Your Management Persona**: Sketch a brief outline of how you will create hope and certainty, take charge, be an admired and respected manager, and incorporate elements of your personality into your management persona. Below is an example based on my own approach. Feel free to use bullet points that resonate with you, but customize them to reflect your unique style and strengths.

  o **Create Hope and Certainty**

    ▪ Stay Positive: Maintain an optimistic outlook about the

company's future and the world.

- Address Uncertainty: Confront and address situations that cause uncertainty directly and promptly.

- Career Path Development: Collaborate with each team member to create a clear career path, providing them with hope and a vision for a bright future within the company.

- **Take Charge**

  - Confrontation and Decision-Making: Utilize newly acquired skills to address situations and make decisions swiftly.

  - Ownership: Take full responsibility for the department's outcomes and the performance of individual team members.

  - Proactive Planning: Identify potential problems and opportunities early and plan and execute initiatives to address both.

o **Be Admired and Respected**

- Kindness: Treat everyone with kindness and respect.

- Integrity: Keep your word and follow through on commitments.

- Improvement Focus: Work diligently to improve the company and enhance your team's work life.

o **Be Yourself**

- Sense of Humor: Incorporate your sense of humor into daily management interactions to foster a positive atmosphere.

- Presenting: Take advantage of opportunities to present to your team and larger company audiences, leveraging your enjoyment of public speaking.

- Personal Connection: Get to know your team members personally, including their

families and individual
aspirations, to build strong,
relatable relationships.

- **Actionable Steps**: For each element of your
  management persona, write down one
  actionable step you can take to strengthen
  that aspect in your professional life. For
  example, how can you use your humor to
  create a more hopeful and confident
  atmosphere for your team?

- **Implement and Adjust**: Implement your
  management persona in your daily
  management practices. After a few weeks,
  reflect on the impact. How has it affected
  your team's morale and performance? What
  adjustments might you need to make?

A FINAL THOUGHT

Finding myself in midtown Manhattan on 9/11 was an
unexpected twist of fate that shaped my outlook on
life, change, and the nature of uncertainty.

As we move forward, we'll delve into a challenge
that was a significant hurdle in my early career and
one I've seen many managers struggle with
throughout my years in management and coaching
individual performance. It's a common stumbling
block, particularly the difficulty in managing day-to-
day activities. The next chapter unpacks the
complexities of that, offering insights and strategies to

navigate this critical aspect of management. Stay tuned.

PART 2: MANAGING OTHERS

CHAPTER 5
MANAGING INDIVIDUAL
PERFORMANCE

You're on the road to conquering confrontation, have begun to make well-thought-out and timely decisions, and are establishing your management persona. These prerequisite skills set you up to succeed in managing others, which starts with managing individual performance. If you don't actively manage individual performance, then a lack of performance is what you will reap.

Let's consider a real-life example before we delve into managing individual performance. This story underscores the importance of proper management training and the impact of proactive management. Years ago, when I was in magazine advertising sales, I watched a peer get promoted. Bobby, a longtime salesperson, was promoted to the role of publisher after the previous one left. He faced multiple challenges. He had never held a management position and received little to no guidance from his boss.

Additionally, the dot-com bubble had just burst, leading to a recession that saw advertisers cutting back. Unsurprisingly, Bobby struggled to manage his people and the magazine. He was a deer in headlights. He didn't confront people situations, he didn't make decisions, and he didn't meet with his people either as a group or individually. In less than a year, he was put back into a sales role, and the magazine was given to a more experienced manager.

This scenario is common: star individual contributors get promoted without proper training and support. Research from CEB Global indicates that 60% of new managers fail within the first 24 months in their new role. Let's explore how to avoid this fate, with the key being managing individual performance.

The Importance of Balancing Compassion and Command in Performance Management

Managing individual performance effectively requires a balance between compassion and command. Compassionate managers may excel at understanding and addressing the personal challenges of their team members but may struggle with administering accountability. On the other hand, commanding managers might enforce standards effectively but could overlook the individual needs and morale of their team. Integrating both approaches to create a balanced and supportive environment that holds people accountable is key.

THE THREE KEYS TO MANAGING INDIVIDUAL PERFORMANCE

Remember your job: to manage yourself and your people to get the job done. You must have a system to effectively manage your people. There are three keys to managing individual performance:

1. The One-on-One Meeting

2. Managing Motivation

3. Assessing and Addressing Stress

Let's explore each of these in detail.

THE ONE-ON-ONE MEETING

One-on-one meetings are crucial for managing individual performance. Regularly meeting with your team helps you stay on top of their progress, address obstacles, and provide necessary support.

Compassionate managers can use these meetings to ensure they are not just offering support but also setting clear expectations and holding their team accountable. Commanding managers should focus on actively listening to their team members and showing empathy, ensuring the meeting is not just about directives but also understanding and support.

Here's a practical agenda for these meetings:

1. **Opening**:

    o Brief check-in: "How's everything in your world today?"

    o This is your employees' time to tell you what's on their mind.

2. **Monitor Their Progress**:

   o   Discuss current tasks and any competing priorities.

   o   Inquire about recent successes and insights gained.

3. **Acknowledge Achievements and Provide Recognition**:

   o   Highlight and congratulate recent achievements.

   o   Discuss the impact of these achievements on the team and company.

4. **Evaluate Goals and Priorities**:

   o   Review key items from prior meetings.

   o   Review and ensure clarity of current goals.

   o   Adjust priorities as needed and check progress.

5. **Address Obstacles to Performance**:

   o   Identify support needed from you or the team.

   o   Brainstorm solutions for current obstacles.

6. **Managing Their Motivation**:

- o Ensure they feel valued.

- o Use emotional currency; examples include: Giving compliments and encouragement, assigning special projects, asking them for help, celebrating victories, taking them into your confidence, and increasing their responsibility. These can be powerful motivators.

- o Autonomy: Empower employees by giving them the freedom to make decisions in their areas of responsibility.

7. **Closing the Meeting**:

- o Recap key points and agreed-upon actions.

- o Set the date and focus for the next meeting.

- o Express appreciation: "I appreciate your contribution and efforts."

I can't overstate the importance of meeting with your people individually regularly. The regularly scheduled one-on-one is the foundation for managing your team's performance. I recommend scheduling meetings every 7–14 days. If you don't meet with your people, you are not managing them. This meeting enables you to hold your people accountable.

A client of mine recently said that I held them accountable positively. They used the phrase positive accountability. That is a wonderful way to look at it. Effectively managing someone is a very positive thing. If you manage your team, you will understand where they allocate their time, their conflicting priorities, what is effective for them, and the obstacles to their success, among other factors. You also know if they are getting the job done. Knowing these things enables you to hold them accountable.

Meeting with them regularly and reviewing business results is a measure of keeping them responsible for their job performance. This is what accountability is. Positive accountability means your genuine motivation and actions focus on improving employee performance and consistently holding people accountable.

It all boils down to always meeting with your people and working through the items on the list and your follow-up notes from prior meetings. Give your people honest feedback—candid feedback is a gift.

Remember that being a role model is essential, as we learned in Chapter Four in the "Be admired and respected" section. You want to be admired and respected, so you had better demonstrate accountability in your actions and decisions and set a precedent for your team regarding how things are done and handled.

MANAGING MOTIVATION

As noted above, managing motivation is a key part of the one-on-one meeting agenda. Still, it's important to emphasize that motivation is not a one-time task and should not be limited to the one-on-one meeting; it's a continuous effort. Managers play a pivotal role in influencing their team's motivation, and understanding the following elements will help you keep your team engaged and motivated:

- **Meaningful Contribution**: Ensure each team member knows how their work impacts the organization's goals.

- **Recognition**: Regularly acknowledge efforts and achievements to foster a positive and motivating work environment.

- **Sense of Belonging**: Communicate that each person is essential to the team's success.

- **Opportunities for Growth**: Encourage continuous learning and career advancement by providing the tools and opportunities needed.

- **Autonomy**: Grant freedom in decision-making, which increases job satisfaction and drives motivation.

- **Emotional Currency**: Utilize non-monetary rewards like compliments, special projects, and increased responsibility to reinforce their value to you, the company, and the team.

COMPASSION And COMMAND

Motivation is most effective when it combines the positive reinforcement typical of compassionate leadership with the clear expectations and standards expected of a commanding approach. Compassionate managers should ensure they are not just providing support but also challenging their team to grow. Commanding managers, conversely, should ensure they motivate not just by setting high standards but also by recognizing and nurturing their team members' individual needs and strengths.

It's also crucial to recognize that there are two primary ways to motivate people: through positive encouragement or through fear-based tactics. While positive motivation—like the above strategies—fosters a supportive and productive environment, negative motivation uses fear as the primary motivator. Reflecting on my experience in the bread business, I worked for a manager named Andy, who relied heavily on negative motivation. His approach was rigid: it was his way or the highway. If you made a mistake or did something he disagreed with, he would threaten to fire you if it happened again. This created a toxic work environment where I constantly feared for my job. After 11 years with that company, I left because I could no longer tolerate Andy's management style. I found a new job with an outstanding boss—one of the best I've ever had—who exemplified positive motivation. I vowed never to use fear to motivate my people and to never again work for a boss who did.

In today's work environment, employees are increasingly unwilling to tolerate working for fear-based managers. I'm confident that you, too, will choose to motivate your team through positive means. Be sure to incorporate positive motivation into your daily routine. Doing so will create a workplace where motivation remains a priority, helping your team stay focused, engaged, and productive.

ASSESSING AND ADDRESSING STRESS

I've witnessed superstar employees become different people and poor performers under stress. Stress, a timeless challenge, can transform personalities. It's essential to recognize the dual nature of everyone's personality: one under normal conditions and another under stress.

As a manager, you'll inevitably face supporting a stressed team member, and balancing compassion and command becomes crucial. Compassionate managers must be empathetic and proactive in helping their team manage stress while maintaining performance standards. Commanding managers should focus on integrating empathy into their approach, recognizing when stress affects performance, and offering appropriate support.

Here's how to address stress in your workplace:

1. **Observe and Acknowledge:** Regular interactions with your team enable you to detect unusual behaviors. Approach these

changes with concern but avoid prying into personal matters.

2. **Provide Support**: There are almost always things a manager can do to temporarily make an employee's work life easier for them. Do what you can. Inform employees about available mental health resources. If stress appears severe, suggest professional help. Drawing from personal experience, I've found that seeking professional advice is very helpful.

3. **Maintain Professional Boundaries:** Empathy is vital, yet maintaining professional interactions and avoiding delving into private issues unrelated to work is important. Many employees will volunteer a lot of information regarding the sources of their stress. Try not to get involved in too many of these details.

4. **Monitor Progress:** During routine one-on-ones, assess the employee's condition while maintaining professionalism. Avoid sharing sensitive details with others, but if necessary, briefly inform your superior that the employee is experiencing stress, underscoring your actions to manage the situation.

Everybody has a healthy behavioral profile and a different one while under stress. You can get an affordable stress behavior profile called Friction EQ at gobeyond.com. This profile can help you and your team better understand individual team members' stress responses. I discuss it further in the resources section at the end of the book.

Remember, every manager will encounter stressed subordinates. These guidelines are designed to help you navigate these challenges effectively. Through my years in management, I learned to handle my stress, improving over time. Learning to effectively deal with stress takes time, not just for your team but also for you. I haven't included a section for managing stress on the One-on-One Agenda because I don't think that's needed. I've covered it sufficiently here, and I'm sure you will be alerted to it.

READER TAKEAWAYS

- **Balancing Compassion and Command**: Effective performance management means balancing understanding your team members' needs and holding them accountable to high standards. Managers who lean too heavily on compassion may struggle to meet expectations, while those who focus solely on authority might miss out on building strong, supportive relationships. The key is to blend both approaches.

- **The Role of One-on-One Meetings**: Regular one-on-one meetings are the cornerstone of managing individual performance. They allow for progress tracking, addressing obstacles, setting clear expectations, and fostering positive accountability.

- **Managing Motivation Continuously**: Motivation isn't a one-time task but an ongoing process combining positive reinforcement and clear expectations.

- **Addressing Stress in the Workplace**: Recognizing and addressing stress is necessary for supporting your team and maintaining performance. Managers must provide support while maintaining professional boundaries, helping employees manage stress without compromising expectations.

CHAPTER EXERCISE

1. **Evaluate Your Current Management Approach**:

   - Consider how you currently manage your team. List areas where you could be more involved or systematic. Reflect on whether you naturally lean toward compassion or command when managing performance.

   - Consider incorporating elements from the opposite approach to create a more balanced management style. For example, a compassionate manager might focus on becoming more assertive in setting and enforcing expectations, while a commanding manager might work on improving their listening skills and offering more personalized support.

2. **List Your Team Members**: Make a list of your direct reports. Next to each name, note any specific management needs or issues you must address.

3. **Set up Your One-on-One Meeting Tracking Tool and Schedule and Conduct Meetings**:

- I like to use Microsoft OneNote for this because it allows you to create an individual section for each team member and then a subsequent "Page" for each one-on-one meeting, but any online tool that will keep you organized is fine. Here's how I set up OneNote:

  o Create a new Notebook and title it "One-on-One Meeting."

  o Create a new section for each direct report.

  o Create a page for your first One-on-One Meeting with each direct report.

- ○ Create a "PROFILE" page for each direct employee and include information specific to them (e.g., their birthday, names of family members, special hobbies—anything specific to them).

- Schedule your one-on-one meetings, but remember not to schedule too many on the same day.

- Conduct the meetings and take notes for any specific items of importance. If you don't take notes, you WILL forget, and these meetings will lose effectiveness.

4. **Adjustment:** After a few meetings, analyze how the meeting went:

- What's working well?

- What needs adjustment?

5. **Continuous Improvement:** Adjust your approach based on your meeting feedback and observations. Managing individual performance is an ongoing process; you must continuously adjust your management style to meet your team's and company's evolving needs.

A FINAL THOUGHT

Managing individual performance involves practical steps to ensure your team members' success. In addition to becoming a foundation for your management, these steps set the stage for your ability to hold your people accountable. In Bobby's story earlier, we noted multiple management failures, chief among them a lack of managing individual performance. Without it, there was no constructive guidance or support to help his team succeed.

Time to time, management requires difficult actions like performance improvement plans or terminations. When you consistently manage individual performance—through regular, supportive check-ins—you create an environment where such drastic steps are less likely to be needed. These steps, which may sometimes be uncomfortable, are necessary management actions. Although difficult actions might not feel positive, they are always better than inaction. Remember that unaddressed negative situations always turn into problems that make you wish you had made a well-thought-out decision and acted on it. While managing individual performance is crucial, not all team members will respond positively.

In the next chapter, we'll explore how to effectively handle problem people, ensuring your team remains on track.

CHAPTER 6
MANAGING PROBLEM PEOPLE

Every manager will face problem people. This is a difficult area and one that can often be unpleasant. Effectively managing problem people requires a delicate balance between compassion and command. Compassionate managers may hesitate to address problematic behavior due to concern for the individual's feelings, while commanding managers might address the issues swiftly but risk overlooking the underlying causes that could be resolved through support and guidance. Both approaches have their strengths, but integrating them leads to more effective management of problem people.

Let's start with a story highlighting the dangers of ignoring problem behavior. Years ago, while in magazine advertising sales, I worked alongside a peer named Tom. The company thought that Tom's behavioral problems would improve if they promoted him, so they did. How do you suppose that turned out? Tom was notorious for a huge list of infractions. He made fun of people with weight problems, people of color, and people in the LGBTQ+ community. You name it, he targeted them. Tom was a big guy who had played college basketball at a major school. He was mean-spirited, intimidating, and a bully. I personally thought he needed to see a mental health professional. Astonishingly, the company, particularly some senior managers, let this out-of-control maniac wield negativity in their halls for over 10 years. He was a disaster. Eventually, they addressed it and fired him.

Have I ever waited too long to deal with a problem person? Sure. But with experience comes wisdom. Over time, I recognized the damage problem people create and became quite good at addressing them head-on.

Dealing with problem people isn't about being harsh. It's about stepping up, setting clear expectations, and refusing to let one person drag the team down.

Problem people hurt you in so many ways. They:

- run off good people
- run off customers
- ruin morale
- take an enormous amount of your time, emotional energy, and resources
- hurt your entire team's overall performance and, in turn, the company's performance.

If you don't proactively manage and hold your problem people accountable for their actions, your good people will lose respect for you. Eventually, your manager will get involved, which means she is doing your job, and that's never good.

Multiple Problem People

Years ago, I took over a region with 21 people on my team. I was beyond astonished to discover that 11 of those people were problem people. This was the most challenging personnel situation I've ever faced, and it took me well over a year to completely sort it out. I started with my first termination 60 days after my arrival.

Every client I have worked with has had problem people in their organization. Some of my senior-level clients don't have direct reports who are problem people, but they have problem people further down in their organizations. I have managed multiple teams with no problem people over the years, but that vaunted status didn't happen by itself. You can absolutely get there. It's rare for an entire company to be problem-people-free.

I recently worked with a client who managed two teams. In total, she had four problem people. She worked on the process we will review next, and three of her problem people resigned, and she terminated the fourth. Managing people who either don't fit the culture or don't get the job done is a fact of management that you need to skill up for.

THE FOUR-CATEGORY EVALUATION

To effectively manage problem people, you first need to complete a simple two-question evaluation for each of your people. You can do this in the exercise at the end of this chapter. Ask yourself these two questions for each of your people:

1. Are they a cultural fit?

2. Do they get the job done?

From there, place your people into one of four categories on the 4-Category Evaluation:

1. **Positive Performers** fit the culture and get the job done.

2. **Negative Performers** don't fit the culture, but they get the job done.

3. **Positive Non-performers** fit the culture but don't get the job done.

4. **Negative Non-performers** don't fit the culture and don't get the job done.

You only want positive performers on your team. Your problem people include everyone else. If someone doesn't fit in, do their job well, or both, they are a problem, and you must take action.

ACCOUNTABILITY TOOLS

The one-on-one meeting you learned about in Chapter 5 will be the primary setting where you will hold your people accountable. This is where 90% of your accountability work will take place. In addition to the regularly scheduled one-on-one, you have many additional accountability tools to work with. Here are my favorites:

1. **Issue-Specific One-on-One**: Follow up in a separate one-on-one meeting focused solely on the issue. This is a great first step for dealing with a problem person who is either not fitting in or not getting the job done. Focus on "Evaluate Goals and Priorities" in Chapter Five's "One-on-One Meeting" section. Make sure the two of you develop clear goals and priorities. You may have to mandate some of these and check in regularly on progress.

2. **Individual Development Plan (IDP)**: Use these when you think your employee can "make it." An IDP can highlight specific goals, training, and skills development for team members who need it. This tool is useful for compassionate managers to set clear expectations while offering support. Commanding managers should use this to provide structured growth opportunities before considering harsher measures.

3. **Performance Improvement Plan (PIP)**: Use these when you don't think your employee can "make it." Document the poor performance by putting the employee on a plan. Work the plan that's spelled out. Most PIPs have a set period, usually 90 days. You don't need to wait 90 days to terminate an

employee if they are not making acceptable progress. Compassionate managers must recognize when it's time to move from support to accountability, while commanding managers should use the PIP to offer a clear final chance for improvement.

4. **Transfer**: Sometimes, transferring a problem employee to a different role can solve the issue. This option works well when the employee fits the culture but struggles in their current role. However, avoid this option if the employee has never performed well.

5. **Suspension**: This is another tool at your disposal, especially when you need more information before making a final decision. Remember that you have the option to either suspend with or without pay. I never suspended anyone without pay, and I recommend you don't either. We will discuss this option in more detail in the next chapter.

6. **Termination**: This is the last step in the accountability process. In most of the terminations I've been involved with, we first used one or more of the above steps. Even when dealing with an explosive situation, I usually suspend the employee first.

CONFRONTING PROBLEM PEOPLE

Here is where we will practice the strategies from Chapter 2, "Conquering Confrontation." Tackling the challenge of difficult team members may feel daunting initially. Still, it's a competence you'll improve with real-world practice. Compassionate managers must stay true to their empathetic nature but avoid becoming distant or indifferent.

It's important to recognize the complexity of these situations and do your planning. Commanding managers may find these conversations more straightforward but should consider the employee's feelings and the impact of the discussion on them.

Regardless of your management style, remember that you hold the power to significantly influence someone's career and life. Guiding them toward a positive path can have tremendous results. The exercise at the end of this chapter gives you a step-by-step approach to evaluating and managing any problem people you may have. The following hands-on example ensures you have the tools and knowledge to manage problem people, which goes a long way toward building a stronger team.

PROBLEM PEOPLE EXAMPLE

Let's assume you've got six direct reports and you've done a 4-Category Evaluation. You've got three

Positive Performers, one Negative Performer, one Positive Non-performer, and one Negative Non-performer. This means you've got three problem people on your team; two are non-performers and are not getting the job done. Not great, but not terrible either. Here is what that looks like:

1. **Positive Performers**: 3 people
2. **Negative Performers**: 1 person
3. **Positive Non-performers**: 1 person
4. **Negative Non-performers**: 1 person

I always recommend managing this from the bottom up. Address the Negative Non-performer first. Consult with your boss and then take action.

ADDRESSING THE NEGATIVE NON-PERFORMER

The Negative Non-performer doesn't fit the culture, i.e., they cause multiple problems with other team members and/or others in the organization and don't get the job done. Compassionate managers may struggle to act because they empathize with the person's challenges, but delaying action only causes more harm. Commanding managers might move too quickly without considering the individual's potential for improvement. The best approach is to create a PIP with weekly check-ins. If performance does not improve after a few weeks regarding job performance and cultural fit, terminate the employee promptly.

ADDRESSING THE POSITIVE NON-PERFORMER

Positive Non-performers fit the culture but don't get the job done. This person is difficult to manage because they try hard, and everyone likes them. Compassionate managers may give them too much time while commanding managers might overlook their growth potential. The solution is to set clear expectations and timelines for improvement. I've had Positive Non-performers who tried hard and who everybody loved. They would show up on time, work all day, always have nice things to say, participate in company events, etc. They are not performing, but you like them. Everybody likes them. You give them extra time to learn the job, have them work with others who can help them, and go above and beyond to try and make it work, and it feels like the right thing to do. If you are an experienced manager, you've seen this. What I've noticed repeatedly is that the manager spends too much time, in some cases years, trying to make this work. You generally find people in three sub-categories here. Let's look at each one in detail.

- ***The New Employee Who is Not Performing:*** Here is my rule: if they are new and do not meet or exceed the minimum standards by 90 days, they will never make it. Never. You should let them go. Depending on the situation, assuming you've already utilized the issue-specific one-on-ones, you should move to the PIP and then to termination when appropriate. Years ago, I had a VP who was new in their role. They hired a business development rep who was just not making it. The VP desperately wanted this new rep to succeed. I let the VP handle it and would regularly inquire about this individual. It took our VP two years to finally decide that this business development rep would not make it. It shouldn't have taken us two years to make this decision. Our VP learned a lesson, and we released a really good person who was then free to chase opportunities where they could excel. Looking back, it's clear that holding on to this rep for two years was unfair to the company and the employee. In upholding my commitment to the VP and letting them manage and make "the decision," I failed both the company and the employee, and that's my fault. But I learned from that experience. Remember the 90-day rule. I don't recommend transferring this person. I've seen people move a new positive non-performer, and I don't recall an instance where that worked out.

- ***The Established Employee Who Has Never Performed:*** I would start with a PIP for this employee. They've been around for a while and likely know they've not been performing. If not, then a PIP allows them to right their ship. Experience tells me that this person will probably not make it. I can't recall a single instance where an established employee who had never met expectations managed to make a turnaround. A PIP is a great and fair way to give them the opportunity, but if that does not work, move to termination.

- ***The Established Employee Who Used to Perform***: If you have an employee who has previously performed in their current or previous roles, you should consider a few options. First, I would meet with the employee and see where their head is. Can they return to where they consistently perform in their current role? If you both think this is possible, then build them an IDP. A PIP is the best next path if that doesn't work. The next option is a transfer or a new role. If your employee possesses other skills or has the potential to develop new ones, and there's a need for them within your company, transferring them to a different department might be a viable solution. I have had some success with this. It's great when you can "save" a good employee; it's good for everybody and great for morale. A company's culture is the people in it. You and your company need all the good people you can find.

Not addressing Positive Non-performers is a problem. What does that do to your job and team's performance and morale? It's easy to let Positive Non-performers linger on your team for too long. You need to guard against that.

ADDRESSING THE NEGATIVE PERFORMER

They don't fit the culture, but they get the job done. They cause problems, and they usually have issues with other people. This group exists in almost every company in America. American businesses have room for people who do the job regardless of the collateral damage they create. You don't want these people on your team. Compassionate managers might hesitate to take action because of the employee's strong performance, while commanding managers may focus solely on their output. Thus, both types of managers tend to wait too long to act on employees in this category.

Work with these people and focus on their destructive behaviors, not their attitudes, and work to correct these bad behaviors. If they don't change, you and your company will be better off without these individuals. I don't have to tell you the damage that problem people in this group can cause to your team and the whole organization. It's hard to get rid of people getting the job done because corporate America always needs to get the job done. I've committed the sin of staying with a negative performer who didn't change for too long more than once. In one particular instance, I had a negative performer who was highly toxic but was a superstar performer. I stayed with them too long, causing my team, company, and myself to suffer the negative consequences of my inaction. I learned a valuable lesson the hard way.

After that experience, I moved quickly on Negative Performers. Years ago, I had a superstar performer in this category who was also a manager. They had consistent conflicts with their direct reports and with other managers. Interestingly, customers loved them. I transferred them to a senior individual contributor role, solving the problem. Many years later, they are still performing well with the same company. I've also been hired to coach people in this category and have had success.

In many cases, it's just a matter of bringing the negative behavior to your employees' attention. This is an interaction that many managers never have, and it goes back to Chapter 2, conquering confrontation. Most, but not all, negative performers create a lot of damage and end up being fired or leaving on their own.

When I think back over 31 years of managing people, I cannot remember having a situation where having an unaddressed Negative Performer on the team had a happy ending. If you have someone on your team who fits this category, you must address it. Remember, you always need performers on your team, but you can't have the kind of disruption that this person is causing. I know what I just wrote is easier said than done, but I'm here to tell you that this problem won't disappear by itself.

POSITIVE PERFORMERS

Positive Performers fit the culture and get the job done. These are the most valuable people on your team. Now that you are doing regular one-on-ones, you can adequately manage and recognize them. This chapter is not about this golden group.

CONFRONTING PROBLEM PEOPLE

Tackling the challenge of difficult team members may feel daunting initially, but it's a competence you'll get better at with real-world practice. If your approach leans toward compassion, staying true to that is crucial—avoid becoming distant or indifferent. Recognizing the complexity of these situations is vital, do your planning. For those with a command-oriented style, these conversations might seem more straightforward. However, you need to consider the employees' feelings and the impact of the discussion on them. Regardless of your management style, remember that you hold the power to significantly influence someone's career life. Guiding them toward a positive path can have tremendous results. The exercise at the end of this chapter gives you a step-by-step approach to evaluating and managing any problem people that you may have. This hands-on approach ensures you have the tools and knowledge to manage problem people, which goes a long way toward building a stronger team.

READER TAKEAWAYS

1. You've probably got one or more problem people on your team. Intuitively, you likely know the situation and what you need to do. Work through the process in the chapter exercise that follows.
2. Problem people hurt themselves, you, your customers, and your company.
3. Familiarize yourself with your accountability tools: issue-specific one-on-ones, IDPs (individual development plans), PIPs (performance improvement plans), transfers, suspensions, and terminations.

CHAPTER EXERCISE

- **Evaluate Your Current Management Approach**: Reflect on your natural tendencies. Are you more compassionate or more commanding when managing problem people? Consider how you can integrate the opposite approach to improve your effectiveness.

- **Assess Your Team**: Using the 4-Category Evaluation from this chapter, categorize your team members as Positive Performers, Negative Performers, Positive Non-performers, or Negative Non-performers.

- **Identify Problem Areas**: Identify specific issues or behaviors that need addressing for

each team member not in the Positive
Performers category. Be as detailed as
possible.

- **Choose Your Accountability Tools**:
  Select appropriate accountability tools for
  each problem team member based on the
  identified issues. This could include issue-
  specific one-on-ones, IDPs, or PIPs.

- **Action Plan Development**: Create a
  detailed action plan for each problem team
  member. This should include your steps,
  timelines, and expected outcomes. The plan
  should include one of the accountability tools,
  such as inside the issue-specific one-on-one,
  the IDP, or PIP.

- **Implement and Monitor**: Begin
  implementing your action plans. Regularly
  monitor the progress of each team member,
  adjusting your approach as necessary based
  on their response and improvement. Be sure
  to take detailed notes inside of an electronic
  platform.

- **Reflect and Adjust**: After a set period,
  reflect on the effectiveness of your approach.
  Consider what worked, what didn't, and how
  you can improve your management of
  problem people in the future.

A Final Thought

Dealing with problem people can be unpleasant, but it will become easier over time. Be sure to consider how much better things will become once the issue is resolved. The longer a problem person is left unaddressed, the more harm they can do—to your team, morale, and overall performance. Tom, the out-of-control manager we discussed early in this chapter, was a classic example. I watched from afar as our company allowed his toxic behavior to persist, hoping it would resolve itself. It didn't. Eventually, it led to his termination, but only after years of damage. Tom's situation is a reminder of the importance of confronting these issues head-on, no matter how difficult it may seem. Tom was more than just a problem person. In Chapter 7, "Explosive Situations: Navigating Personnel Crises," we will explore this special subset that occasionally arises from problem people.

CHAPTER 7
NAVIGATING EXPLOSIVE SITUATIONS

Explosive situations are challenging for many reasons, chief among them being that, as a new manager, you've likely never faced anything like them. These one-off, out-of-the-blue crises can leave even the most experienced managers unprepared. Take heart—this chapter will show you the light. I wish I had access to this guidance as a new manager.

Effectively managing explosive situations requires a balance between compassion and command. Compassionate managers may focus on the emotional impact on those involved, potentially delaying necessary decisive actions. Commanding managers might prioritize swift, clear decisions but risk overlooking the emotional complexities that could exacerbate the situation. Both approaches have strengths, but integrating them leads to a more effective resolution.

Let's dive into a situation I helped a client company work through. Becky, a department manager at one of my client companies, was involved in a relationship with the estranged husband of one of her employees, Paula. The entire department was in an uproar. With over 40 people in the department, virtually everyone sided with Paula, leaving Becky isolated. To make matters worse, the husband had made threats against some people in the department. I advised my client to hire an off-duty sheriff's deputy to patrol their parking lot during business hours for two weeks.

Additionally, they upgraded their door security and suspended Becky with pay until a decision could be made. Ultimately, the company determined that Becky's romantic involvement with an employee's husband had alienated her from her team, rendering her ineffective in her management role. She was given severance and let go.

This situation highlights how explosive scenarios often require decisive action (command) and empathy for those involved (compassion). The department returned to normal as soon as the company took action. The one-off nature of these situations makes them challenging. If you manage a large organization, you'll occasionally face volatile scenarios. No management book or Harvard Business case study can fully prepare you for this. However, the tools outlined in this chapter will help you navigate these crises effectively by blending compassion and command.

REAL-WORLD EXAMPLES

I hate to even write this section, but it reflects the reality of our world. Over my career, I've encountered more explosive situations than I care to remember, both personally and with client companies. While it's impossible to say you've seen it all, I group these incidents and put them in one category called "Explosive Situations." Although there is a never-ending variety of Explosive Situations, nearly all can be handled using the tools we'll explore in this chapter.

Here are a few examples:

- I had an employee secretly record a confidential, high-level meeting and use the recording to influence and intimidate another employee.

- I've had multiple people steal money from the company.

- I had an intoxicated employee point a handgun at another employee at a company party. That same employee was also accused of other serious offenses in the workplace.

- I've dealt with employees' spouses making threats against our staff, including one who owned multiple firearms and showed up in our parking lot looking for a manager involved with their estranged spouse.

- I had the friend of an employee message me, telling me that one of my employees had threatened suicide the night before.

- I worked with a junior manager who was concerned that firing a "negative non-performing" employee could lead to violent retaliation.

Each of these examples required a compassionate understanding of the individuals involved and commanding decisive action to ensure the safety and stability of the workplace. As we discuss the tools to manage these situations, we'll see how balancing these approaches leads to better outcomes.

THE TOOLS TO USE

When faced with an explosive situation, your natural inclination toward compassion or command will influence your initial response. However, these situations are serious and leave no room for inaction. By blending compassion and command, you can navigate these crises more effectively. Here are the tools you should use:

1. **Your Boss and HR Department**: Your boss must know about every potentially explosive or explosive situation immediately. Do whatever you can to make that communication happen. Still, depending on the situation, you may need to act before hearing back from them. You must quickly evaluate the situation and make your best judgment. If you can confer with your boss and/or HR department, they may have a good

option for you, but if you're stumped, I offer the following additional tools, which you should use in conjunction with your superiors. The list below was built from my years of experience.

2. **Immediate Termination**: In the case of the secretly recorded board meeting, and when I discovered employees stealing, the answer was immediate termination. There is a long list of things that generally call for immediate termination. This is just a guideline; be sure to follow company policy. Since this is a first-time manager's handbook, here are some behaviors that generally require immediate termination:

- violence or threats of violence
- theft or fraud
- substance abuse
- harassment or discrimination
- serious misconduct that violates company policy
- insubordination (willful refusal to follow legitimate orders from superiors)
- deliberate actions that compromise workplace safety
- criminal activity
- misuse of company resources (using resources for personal gain).

Collect your facts, present your evidence to the employee, and terminate them from the company. We will discuss termination in detail in the next chapter.

3. **Suspension with Pay**: This is an excellent tool, and you need to be aware that you have this option when needed. I've only used it a handful of times over my career, but it quickly calms down a situation and gives you time to regroup, investigate, confer with counsel, and decide. Since you are suspending someone with pay, you are not imposing financial hardship on the employee, so it's easy to execute.

In the instance when I had an employee with a handgun who was also accused of other serious offenses in the workplace, I didn't witness any of this. Our policy manual dictates an investigation for all accusations of this nature. The first move was to suspend the employee, which I did immediately upon hearing about this situation. This was followed by hiring a reasonably priced HR consultant to help us conduct an internal investigation. The board was informed, and since a gun was involved, they recommended additional security. We hired an off-duty sheriff's deputy to monitor our office during office hours and at the end of the day. We did this for two weeks, and there was never a problem. The investigation process took two weeks to finish, after which I met the suspended employee at a restaurant for coffee and terminated them. Until this crazy situation, I had a good working relationship with this individual, so a month later, I took them to lunch and did my best to give them career advice, letting my compassionate manager side come through.

In every case, when I suspended someone with pay, the situation ended in termination. Suspension with pay is an excellent tool because when you have an explosive situation, you don't always have enough information to proceed directly to termination. You could also suspend someone without pay, but I never liked the punitive nature of that and didn't want to potentially exacerbate an already explosive situation. The employee knows this will likely lead to termination. I always wanted to be as kind and accommodating as possible during this process.

4. **Law Enforcement**: In cases where I was aware of active threats against employees from spouses, I hired an off-duty sheriff's deputy to monitor our office in the mornings when office hours began and again at the end of the day for a few weeks. I have only used this tool three times in my career, and we

have never had any trouble. It was easy and not that expensive. The first time, the head of my HR department and I briefly met with the officer, who just needed a description of the person. The officer said, "You won't even know I'm here." I hope you never have to use this option, but it is an available tool. I have a former colleague who, while at a different company, hired security to be present during a particularly challenging termination. This is another option for you. I never went to that length; we will discuss "The Explosive Situation Termination" in greater detail in the next chapter.

5. **Legal Counsel**: In the case where a friend of an employee whom I did not know messaged me on LinkedIn and told me that an employee had threatened suicide, I didn't know what to do. I thought the LinkedIn message was a hoax, but I messaged the friend. They responded, and I determined it was legitimate. I had no idea how to handle this, so I called our employment lawyer, but she wasn't available. I explained the situation to the receptionist, and they put me on hold. Within 30 seconds, another partner in the law firm was on the phone with me. He told me I was legally bound to act since I knew the situation. This employee worked in a remote two-person office in another state. Ultimately, I had the senior person in that

office take the employee to the employee's brother, who assumed charge and saw that our employee got help. Fortunately, this employee received help. Legal counsel and counsel from your human resources department can be very valuable. As a first-time manager, you won't have direct access to legal counsel, so use your HR department and recommend that they seek legal counsel when unsure of a course of action.

6. **Severance**: I've used severance pay a lot over the years. I never like throwing someone on the street without some temporary support. When the junior manager was concerned that a "negative non-performing" employee would resort to workplace violence if fired, we used severance. This employee was not doing their job and creating stress in the company location. The manager did not want to offer any severance at all in the case where I had an employee with a handgun, mentioned earlier, who was also accused of other serious policy violations; a senior board member advised against severance. I did not take the "no severance" advice in either instance. In the first instance, my manager wanted to wait. We waited. After a month, we developed a tactful, well-thought-out termination process. We met with the employee and candidly communicated that the job's lack of challenge was apparent, and

they were visually disengaged and dissatisfied. Acknowledging their need for more stimulating work, they were encouraged to seek opportunities that matched their aspirations. We offered a generous severance package, ensuring it was balanced and fair, but we didn't go overboard. In the case of the employee with the gun, I gave the employee more severance than they deserved, and my HR consultant agreed.

People don't make rational decisions in emotionally charged situations. Anything you can do to calm the emotions and make life easier for the employee is in your and your company's best interest. Use severance to your advantage when you can. Look at it as a tool. Your company may have strict policies regarding severance, but if you've got an extenuating circumstance, make that known and work to reach an exception. There are always exceptions to rules, especially in explosive situations.

MANAGING EXPLOSIVE SITUATIONS

Handling explosive situations, regardless of your natural management style, is remarkably straightforward when approached with compassion and command. These severe crises require swift, decisive action while considering the emotional and human elements. Compassionate managers must take decisive action when needed while commanding managers should not neglect the human aspect of these crises. Often, these situations end in resignation or termination, but how you get to that outcome matters.

READER TAKEAWAYS

1. **Recognize the Uniqueness of Explosive Situations**: Explosive situations are unique and often require immediate, decisive action. Being prepared for their unpredictability is vital.

2. **Importance of Quick Action**: Act swiftly to de-escalate potentially volatile situations. Tools like paid suspension can be practical in immediately reducing tension.

3. **Communication with Higher Management and HR**: Always inform your boss and HR department about any explosive situation. Their guidance can be invaluable in handling complex scenarios.

4. **Legal and Safety Considerations**: Don't hesitate to seek legal counsel or involve law enforcement in cases involving threats or legal complexities. Safety and legal compliance should be top priorities.

5. **Severance as a Tool**: Consider using severance pay in termination scenarios, especially in sensitive cases. It can help ease the transition and reduce potential backlash.

6. **Learning from Every Situation**: Use each explosive situation as a learning experience. Consider what strategies worked, what could be improved, and how to better handle future incidents.

CHAPTER EXERCISES

Part 1: Evaluate Your Default Approach

1. Reflect on whether you naturally lean more toward compassion or command in managing explosive situations.

2. How has this affected your handling of past crises?

3. Consider how integrating elements from the opposite approach could improve your effectiveness.

Part 2: What Would You Do?

Here's a scenario: You are a district manager for a bread company. You keep getting complaints from a big-box store deli that regularly criticizes the service they receive from one of your breadmen. After investigating, you determine that the complaints are racially motivated and your breadman is being discriminated against. This is a national customer; you can't simply drop the account. How do you handle this?

This scenario calls for balancing compassion (protecting your employee) and command (maintaining the business relationship). After completing your answers to the following questions, compare them with how I handled the situation.

1. What are your goals for this situation?

2. What are your options?

3. What actions will you take?

My primary goal was to protect my employee from an abusive situation. My options included: 1) trying to get the breadman to fix the problem, 2) taking the breadman off this account, or 3) confronting the big-box store deli manager and telling them that I thought their complaint was racially motivated. My solution: I restructured the routes and transferred the big-box deli to another breadman. While it felt like I was rewarding the deli's bad behavior, my concern for my employee's well-being guided my decision. The complaints stopped immediately.

A Final Thought

Because of the experiences in my senior leadership career, I was able to properly advise my client in the story about Becky that opened this chapter. When I first became a senior leader, we had a Chief Operating Officer who was a master at dealing with explosive situations. He taught me the value of using paid suspension to immediately de-escalate an explosive situation. Before working with him, the thought of using a paid suspension never crossed my mind.

I learned a lot from him. Most explosive situations end in termination. If you're currently dealing with such a situation and need guidance on termination, there's an "Explosive Situation Termination" section in the next chapter. I encourage you to reference it now.

CHAPTER 8
FIRING: MANAGING DEPARTURES

It was the worst termination of my career. I was young and inexperienced, a district manager in the bread business, and we suspected that one of our route salesmen was stealing money from the company. There are a variety of ways to steal on a bread route. We tracked this individual's cash receipts and deposits for several months to get to the heart of the matter. He started by pocketing what amounted to lunch money—enough for Burger King a few days a week. Eventually, he escalated to taking 100% of the cash he collected, which added up to about $200 a week. I performed the termination with the help of another junior district manager, so there we were— two managers who didn't know what they were doing. It was an agonizing, hour-long meeting.

Six months later, that same manager and I attended a corporate management training class on "How to Terminate an Employee." When we met in the hall afterward, all we could talk about was how much we wished we'd had that class before that termination. Knowledge and experience save a lot of pain for everyone.

Terminations are brutal, and they require a balance between compassion and command. Compassionate managers may struggle with the emotional weight of a termination, while commanding managers might focus solely on the logistics, potentially overlooking the human side of the process. Navigating terminations effectively means recognizing the strengths and pitfalls of both approaches and integrating them to ensure a humane and decisive process.

Before we dive into the mechanics of terminations, remember that you must comply with your state laws and company's policies if you have them. Your HR person or senior management team can be of great value here, but in my experience, the degree to which they add value varies widely between companies. They generally don't offer much guidance on what to say during a termination; that's where this chapter comes in.

BALANCING YOUR APPROACH

Whether your management style leans toward compassion or command, terminations require a balance of both.

- **For the Compassionate Manager**: Recognize the strength in your empathy. Your natural inclination to understand and share the feelings of others can be an asset during terminations. Lead with kindness and clarity, ensuring the individual understands the decision while feeling supported. However, it's crucial to maintain professional boundaries—your compassion should not hinder the necessary outcome of the termination.

- **For the Commanding Manager**: Your decisiveness and take-charge nature are valuable in making tough decisions clear and straightforward. Yet, it's important to remember the profound effect a termination can have on an individual. Deliver your message with empathy that respects the person's dignity. Offer support through resources or guidance for their next steps, demonstrating that, despite the decision, you wish them well in their future endeavors.

In both cases, preparation is critical. The following sections detail how to plan and execute terminations, guiding you to manage this challenge with compassion and command. Handling terminations with these principles can set a positive example for your team, showing that tough decisions are made with fairness, respect, and integrity.

FIRING

In Chapter 2, you learned how to manage confrontation. One of the most challenging confrontations is employee termination. Even CEOs of the world's largest corporations struggle with termination. It's humiliating to be fired, and at the same time, nobody wants to put a person through that experience. We cover termination in this chapter and define a repeatable process. I've heard that a good manager should hate to fire employees but should not be in a manager's role if they enjoy it or can't do it. I agree with this. I have more experience terminating employees than I wish I did; as with anything, the more you do something, the better you get. If you are new to management and have little to no experience regarding terminations, it's common for an upcoming termination to be your last thought before you go to bed and the first thought that pops into your head when you wake up. You should know that it's normal to dread this. It gets easier over time. Ideally, you will never have to deal with a termination, but that is not reality. Hopefully, you won't have to be involved in many terminations in your career. That means you won't get much experience in this management aspect; if that's the case, I hope this chapter is of great value to you.

HOW DO YOU KNOW?

One of a manager's most challenging decisions is knowing when to terminate someone. A great test I've heard of and used is this: If the person in question came to you today and resigned, would you feel relieved or stressed about losing them? If you feel relieved, it's a sign that it's time for them to go. Use the 4-Box Evaluation tool you learned about in Chapter 6 to quantify your decision.

Unless it's an explosive situation, you and your boss have likely discussed this at length. Now, it's time to execute the termination with a balanced approach.

PLAN THE 'IN-PERSON' TERMINATION

Here's the plan I used for in-person terminations. Use it as a guideline for your own unique situation:

1. **Approvals and HR Notification**: Secure any authorization you need before proceeding. Ensure your HR department is ready with all necessary documentation before continuing. This includes a legally binding agreement detailing the conditions related to the severance package, which the employee may rescind within a certain period post-signing.

2. **Scheduling the Meeting**: Choose a neutral day for the meeting, avoiding significant holidays to ensure minimal disruption. Scheduling it for 11:45 AM is ideal, as it allows the situation to be addressed discreetly during lunch hours.

3. **Selecting the Venue**: Conduct the meeting in a neutral space like a conference room to prevent associating a manager's office with negative experiences. The environment should be professional but not cold.

4. **Who Should Attend**: Ideally, have no more than two people in the room. The direct manager and their supervisor should suffice. Avoid creating a "firing squad" atmosphere, which can be humiliating.

5. **Severance Considerations**: Decide if you will offer severance. While some companies have policies regarding this, severance is often a humane way to treat people. If you can manage it, do it. Additionally, consider offering a placement service to help the employee find a new job—this can make a significant difference in their transition. If I had my career in management to do over again, I would secure a placement program for all terminated employees.

6. **Write and Memorize Your First Sentences**: Start with: "Morgan, you've not made acceptable progress on your performance improvement plan, so we've decided it's time for you to leave Acme Company." If it works for you and your company and you both are okay with offering options, follow with: "We want to help you make this transition as smooth as possible, so we would like your input on how you want this process to transpire."

7. **Offering Options**: If possible, give the employee some control over the process to ease the sting of the termination. If appropriate and permissible, plan on giving them the option of leaving today or working for a week or two. Ask if they want to frame this as a resignation and if they want to notify the team that they are leaving in, say, a week.

Consider any other options you can give them; perhaps they must complete work to help with the transition or share knowledge with a peer. Involving the employee in the process minimizes indignity and helps them retain a sense of control.

CONDUCTING THE TERMINATION MEETING

Now that you've prepared, it's time to conduct the meeting. Whether your natural style leans toward compassion or command, balance is key.

1. **Setting the Room**: The senior person should be in the conference room beforehand. When ready, tell the employee you need to speak with them for a minute and have them follow you. They will probably assume it's a termination meeting when they walk in.

2. **Responsibility**: Managers tend to apologize to the terminated employee. Current HR protocol is to avoid that because it places blame on the company and tends to send a signal that you've done something wrong. I agree with this and now advise people to replace the phrase "I'm sorry" with "This is unfortunate" when discussing the event at hand. Another option is to say, "I hate that it's come to this."

3. **Delivering the Message**: Begin with, "Morgan, unfortunately, you haven't met the expectations outlined in your performance

improvement plan, and we've decided it's time for you to leave Acme Company." Pause for a few seconds to let them process the news. While this moment is never easy, managing it with empathy and authority is crucial. If the employee doesn't respond after a brief pause, continue, "It's unfortunate, but this is where we are, and we need to move forward." Follow this by offering support: "We want to help make this transition as smooth as possible, so we would like your input on how you'd like to proceed." Most employees accept the situation and start thinking about their next steps.

4. **Your Position if Challenged**: The termination meeting is not the place to discuss performance details or argue. The decision is final, and the meeting should focus on how to move forward. Hold the line with firmness but avoid unnecessary confrontation.

5. **Common Questions**: Be ready to answer common questions, such as:

   o **Why am I being terminated?** Restate the primary reason succinctly.

   o **Can I have another chance?** Firmly but kindly explain that the decision is final.

- ○ **What happens to my benefits?**
  Provide information about severance,
  continuation of benefits, and how to
  handle retirement plans, or refer them
  to HR for details.

- ○ **How will this affect my
  references?** Reassure them that you
  will focus on their strengths while
  being honest and professional.

6. **Company Property**: Arrange to collect
   company property, such as electronics,
   company credit cards, or keys.

7. **Closing the Meeting**: Conclude with, "Pat
   (an HR person) has the separation paperwork
   ready in their office. Do you have any
   questions?" End compassionately: "I wish you
   success in the future. It may take time, but
   I'm confident you'll find it." Depending on the
   situation, you might add, "Although this
   didn't work out as we hoped, I appreciate
   your contributions to Acme Company."

ONLINE TERMINATION

Terminating someone over the phone or via an online
meeting platform would have been unacceptable in
the past—it was seen as cold, callous, and cowardly,
something that only "big" impersonal organizations
did. However, with the shift toward remote work,
online terminations have become more common and,

when handled correctly, can be done with both compassion and command.

Follow the same process outlined for in-person terminations, with minor adjustments for the virtual setting:

1. **Time and Location**: Schedule the online meeting when the employee is likely to be in a comfortable and private setting. The senior person should be present when the employee joins the call. The employee might sense that something is wrong when they see their boss's boss or an HR person on the call, but this also happens in in-person terminations.

2. **The Meeting**: Conduct the meeting just as you would in person. While it's easier to be emotionally distant in a virtual setting, strive to maintain empathy by acknowledging the difficulty of the conversation and expressing regret that the situation has come to this.

3. **Advantages of Online Termination**: Online terminations can be easier for the employee because they don't have to deal with the potential humiliation of packing up their things in front of colleagues. It's a more private experience, which can be less emotionally taxing.

THE EXPLOSIVE SITUATION TERMINATION: BLENDING URGENCY WITH EMPATHY

Before terminating an employee responsible for creating an explosive situation, review the tools you have at your disposal, as outlined in Chapter 6:

- Your boss and HR department

- Suspension with pay

- Law enforcement

- Legal counsel

- Severance.

Every situation is different; the above tools will help you manage the process with both compassion and command. Explosive situation terminations generally transpire in two ways—immediate termination or termination after a suspension.

The Immediate Termination: In most cases, personal safety won't be a concern, so you can arrange a meeting with the employee as soon as possible. If possible, have the employee, yourself, and your boss in the room.

Follow this process for the immediate termination associated with an explosive situation:

1. Secure approval for immediate termination from either your boss or HR.

2. Write your first few sentences that briefly recount the situation, including that their actions are unacceptable, that you are letting them go, and that today is their last day.

3. If the employee becomes emotional or upset, remain calm and compassionate but focus on the facts.

4. Do not offer options.

5. If they have questions you are unsure of, you should tell the employee you will get an answer and get back to them.

6. If you need to collect company property from them, do so. Also, inquire about any personal belongings they must take with them.

7. End the meeting by saying: "This is an unfortunate situation. I wish you only the best going forward. I'll be in touch by the end of the day tomorrow regarding the separation paperwork." Since this is immediate, the HR paperwork has probably not been prepared.

If you have a safety concern, plan accordingly. Multiple people in the room are usually enough, but if you're still concerned, consider hiring an off-duty sheriff's deputy to be present. They can be in uniform or plain clothes to minimize disruption.

THE EXPLOSIVE SITUATION TERMINATION AFTER A SUSPENSION

If the employee has been suspended, the termination meeting will likely be more straightforward, but you should still balance empathy with authority. Reach out to the employee and set up a time for them to come in. If they ask whether they are being fired, be honest but compassionate: "Unfortunately, yes." The remainder of the meeting should mirror the process outlined in "The Immediate Termination Associated with an Explosive Situation," except you should have the HR paperwork available. Some employees won't show up for this meeting, and your HR department will likely have a protocol for handling this. Most employees do show up, especially if money is involved.

LAYOFFS: TRANSPARENCY WITH COMPASSION

In my 31 years in management, I've been fortunate to have only one layoff experience. During a national crisis, I had to lay off multiple people. I hated it. I was new to the layoff process and consulted with experienced leaders, but I still didn't handle it as well as I could have. I held one-on-one meetings with each affected employee, which took most of the day. I was too focused on the remaining employees' morale and not enough on those I laid off. I was subsequently accused of not being transparent before the layoffs by at least one person I laid off, and that bothered me.

While layoffs are often unavoidable, transparency is key. Earlier in my career, I worked for a CEO who laid off 125 of our 600 employees over six months. He announced midway through the process that the layoffs were not finished. At the time, I thought he was wrong to instill fear across the company. However, in hindsight, his transparency was the right approach. If layoffs are unavoidable, be open, candid, and transparent. People will stress, but honesty is better than secrecy.

THE EXCEPTIONS: WHEN I TERMINATED PEOPLE ALONE

HR generally wants more than one manager present during a termination meeting. However, I've had a few one-on-one termination meetings over the years, always for the same reason: I had a long-term, personal relationship with the individual, and I wasn't going to handle this like some generic, sterile, and potentially heartless meeting. Adding other people to the meeting makes it less personal, and I wanted to communicate that this was personal. In these cases, a balance of compassion and command was crucial—I needed to convey the decision firmly while honoring our relationship and respecting their dignity.

TRANSPARENCY WITH REASSURANCE

After a termination, it's natural for the remaining team members to feel concerned about their job security and the company's overall stability.

Maintaining transparency while respecting the terminated individual's privacy is essential to avoid creating a perception of randomness or unfairness. How you handle this communication will depend on the nature of the termination.

Suppose the terminated employee was widely regarded as a "problem person," their departure might be anticipated and not cause much concern. Addressing the situation with a brief announcement is likely sufficient in such cases. You can follow your announcement by advising your team that if anyone has any questions, you will address them individually.

If the terminated employee was well-liked or respected, being more proactive is wise. Meet one-on-one with select employees to discuss any concerns. They often express their awareness of the individual's struggles and appreciate how the company handled the situation. Occasionally, someone might be caught off guard. In these cases, explain that while the termination may seem sudden to them, it was not sudden for the individual involved, and efforts were made over time to address the issues. Additionally, it's important to ensure that the workload on your team does not significantly increase while you are short a person. Managers have many levers they can use to adjust the workload, including:

- Personally taking on some of the workload yourself
- Reassigning tasks across the team based on capacity
- Outsourcing or hiring temporary help

- Adjusting deadlines where possible and postponing special initiatives
- Reducing meetings

MANAGING THE "AM I BEING FIRED?" QUESTION

Occasionally, you may find yourself heading into a termination meeting where the employee proactively asks, "Am I going to be fired?" In such cases, you should be prepared to respond with a simple, "Yes, I regret that we are in this situation" or "Unfortunately, that's right." These responses convey the necessary firmness while acknowledging the difficult nature of the conversation.

READER TAKEAWAYS

1. **Preparation is Key**: Ensure you're well-prepared for a termination meeting. This includes understanding the reasons for termination, being clear about company policies and state laws, and anticipating potential reactions.

2. **Handling Terminations with Professionalism and Empathy**: Approach each termination with professionalism and empathy. Recognize the impact on the individual while maintaining the necessary boundaries and clarity. If possible, involve

the employee in the process and give them options for how and when to leave.

3. **Clear and Concise Communication**: Communicate the decision clearly and concisely. Avoid unnecessary details that could lead to confusion or prolong the meeting.

4. **Support for Remaining Team Members**: Plan for post-termination management. This includes how you'll communicate the change to your team and manage any resulting shifts in workload or team dynamics.

CHAPTER EXERCISE

1. **Reflect on Your Experience**: Think about your past experience with terminations. What went well? What could have been improved? Write down these experiences.

2. **Scenario Construction**: The odds are you have a problem person on your team. You may not need to move to terminate this individual but plan for it now so you will be ready if that step becomes necessary. This will be an excellent exercise for you. Consider the reasons for termination and how they align with your company's policies.

3. **Plan the Termination Meeting**: Using the guidelines from this chapter, outline how you would conduct the termination meeting. Include details like the setting, time, who should be present, and critical points to cover, including your first few sentences.

4. **Practice Your Approach**: Role-play the termination scenario with a trusted colleague or mentor. Focus on delivering the message with clarity, empathy, and respect for the individual.

5. **Feedback and Learning**: After the role-play, discuss what went well and what could be improved. Use this feedback to refine your approach to handling such sensitive situations.

6. **Develop a Post-Termination Plan**: Outline how you would handle the aftermath of the termination within your team. Consider aspects like communicating with the remaining team members, addressing workflow changes, and providing support where needed.

A Final Thought

That difficult termination at the beginning of this chapter taught me the importance of knowledge and preparation. It highlighted the need for both compassion and command. I had compassion, but I lacked command. As we turn the page from managing departures to welcoming new talent in Chapter 9, "Hiring," we carry forward these lessons to ensure we not only part ways with dignity but also onboard with foresight, setting the stage for a team's success.

CHAPTER 9
HIRING: MINIMIZING MIS-HIRES

In the previous chapter, we explored the complexities of terminating employees—a process that, even when well-executed, is never pleasant. Following a termination, you often face the challenge of finding a replacement. This presents an opportunity to bring someone into the organization who can make a positive impact, add significant value, and be a pleasure to work with. Many of the world's most successful organizations attribute their success to attracting and retaining top talent, but I can't overstate the importance of hiring. It's challenging to get this right, and I, along with many others, have made a lot of bad hires. As the following story illustrates, job candidates are masters at telling you what they think you want to hear and hiding aspects of themselves that they don't want you to see.

We were growing and needed staff in multiple departments. Our marketing department had four people, and we wanted to add two more. We decided to hire one and onboard them first; after they were up and running, we would try to hire a second person. We figured there would be about six months between the two hires. After interviewing multiple candidates over several weeks, we narrowed the field to two. We loved them both. The first candidate was young; this would only be their second job out of college. Although they had limited work experience, it appeared relevant, and they were a great interviewee. They had also attended a prestigious university on an academic scholarship. The second candidate was older and reentering the workforce after multiple years at home raising children. We decided on the first candidate and hired them. Internally, we continued to discuss the second candidate, fearing they would get another job soon and we'd miss a great opportunity. A week later, we decided to hire for the second position earlier than planned and brought the second candidate on board.

You can probably guess where this is going. The first candidate, who we had chosen as our top pick out of 150 resumes and after a multi-month process, turned out to be a dud—a problem person. Ultimately, they were placed on a performance improvement plan and left the company. The second candidate, on the other hand, became a senior VP within the company. This experience taught me that people will fool you, just like how a produce manager can hide undesirable strawberries in the middle of a container. Not only will candidates hide things, but some will lie in interviews and resumes.

In another situation, we were desperate to fill an IT role. We had an interesting candidate who seemed promising, but we were uncomfortable with the number of jobs this individual had held. While career mobility and multiple jobs are more common today than back when I entered the workforce, this candidate's job history was extreme, with their last two jobs lasting less than six months each. When we asked for references, the candidate refused to provide any and couldn't explain why. We knew why. This chapter is designed to help you avoid situations like these by improving your hiring process.

INFLUENCING HIRING DECISIONS

Whether it leans toward compassion or command, your management style is pivotal in perceiving and evaluating potential candidates. Compassionate managers tend to see the potential in people. They excel at identifying candidates with the drive and adaptability to grow into the role, even if their resume isn't perfect. This perspective is invaluable, especially when considering candidates with non-traditional backgrounds or those reentering the workforce, as it opens the door to diverse talents and unique skill sets.

Conversely, command-oriented managers prioritize decisiveness and proven track records, focusing on candidates with established experience and the ability to hit the ground running. While this approach effectively identifies strong performers, it may overlook candidates with significant potential but less experience. The best approach is to incorporate the strengths each style brings to the table:

- **Compassion** allows you to consider a broader range of candidates, encouraging diversity and uncovering diamonds in the rough, which can yield excellent results.

- **Command** ensures your team remains focused on performance and immediate contributions, which is crucial for roles demanding specific expertise or experience.

The goal is to build a team of individuals who excel independently and enhance each other's strengths. Integrating compassion and command into hiring decisions leads to a more dynamic, resilient, and successful team.

BUILDING A GREAT TEAM

I've worked for multiple companies that didn't trust their HR departments to run the hiring process. Your HR department may have a great hiring system. If they do, run with it, but in my experience, you can't leave this to chance. You live and die by the quality of your team; make sure you are on top of the hiring process. I never thought I was great at hiring, but I built great teams with great people. My struggle was that I made too many mis-hires along the way. My mistakes can be your roadmap to avoiding similar pitfalls.

According to Brad and Geoff Smart, authors of *Topgrading: How to Hire, Coach, and Keep A-*

Players, "The average cost of mis-hiring can be 15 times base salary." When you consider the cost of a mis-hire, it makes all the sense in the world to invest seriously in the hiring process. I've hired hundreds of people over my career and never found a foolproof system, but I did get better over time, and you can, too.

You must understand that you need multiple sources for new hires. I've divided hiring sources into two groups: Primary Sources—a list of sources that gave me the highest percentage of success—and Secondary Sources, a list of sources you need to use to augment your process. Although you won't make as many hires from secondary sources as from primary sources, you will find opportunities there and need to manage and take advantage of those. Your Primary and Secondary Sources will vary based on multiple factors, including your company's location and size, your industry, your budget, the available network and referrals, and the talent pool for the job you are hiring for.

PRIMARY SOURCES: THE FOUNDATION OF YOUR HIRING PROCESS

1. **Hiring someone you've previously worked with** offers a high percentage of success. The person is a known quantity, and you know firsthand their capabilities. I've made some tremendous hires in this category but also made mistakes. Remember, this

person comes in under your reputation, and their performance will reflect on you.

2. **Hiring someone presented by a recruiter** who has done a retained search for you is another reliable option. A recruiter with an exclusive contract has your best interests at heart because they want repeat business. In my last senior management role, we used a recruiter to help us find salespeople, customer success reps, marketing people, and technical services reps. This recruiter hired seven great people for us, and eight years later, all seven are still with the company. I firmly believe in having a good recruiter.

3. **Hiring a customer** can also be highly effective. You know this individual or someone in your company has a relationship with them. The customer understands your industry and knows your product. Over 20 years, I hired customers at two companies, each bringing significant value. I would hire them again if given the chance.

4. **Hiring someone recommended by an industry colleague** or someone you know is another viable source. While these hires can be successful, it's essential to be objective. Is your colleague genuinely trying to help you, the candidate, or both? Many

great—and not-so-great—people get jobs this way. Approach these recommendations with an open mind but maintain a fair and thorough assessment process.

SECONDARY SOURCES: BALANCING RISK AND REWARD

Secondary sources can yield great hires, but they tend to have a lower success rate, which is why I consider them secondary. Nonetheless, they are worth considering, especially when your primary sources aren't delivering the right candidates. As I mentioned, your primary and secondary sources will vary.

1. **Hiring someone a team member has previously worked with** can be terrific or terrible. When it fails, it often results from personal relationships overshadowing professional expectations. I once hired several people from the same company based on one person's recommendation. This group formed their own clique and never integrated into the organization. Eventually, they all left. After that experience, I vowed never to hire more than two people from the same company. I've made good and bad hires from this category, so be diligent in your evaluation.

2. **Hiring someone a team member knows** but hasn't worked with can also be hit or miss. When it fails, it's usually because the

person can't do the job. In most cases where this does not work out, this type of hire results in a Positive Non-performer—someone well-liked but not suited to the role. This can also be great. At my last company, I hired a star performer from this category. Like all categories, remember to be objective.

3. **Hiring someone recommended by an executive** in your company is common, but evaluating these candidates objectively is essential. Executives often try to help the company and someone they know who needs a job. However, these recommendations can carry undue influence. I recall an executive recommending a failed golf pro for a software sales role. I took the candidate to lunch and quickly realized they wanted a career in the golf industry, not software sales. While executives want to help, it's crucial not to give these candidates special consideration based solely on who recommended them.

4. **Explore other platforms** like LinkedIn, indeed, and other specialized job boards, including those in academia. However, my experience has shown that while these resources are valuable, they haven't been as reliable as the methods outlined in the Primary Sources section and the previously mentioned Secondary Sources.

Your industry is different, and your primary and secondary sources will be unique to your company. They may overlap with the ones that worked for me, but they won't be identical.

THE INTERVIEW: BALANCING POTENTIAL AND PROVEN PERFORMANCE

The interview is where you assess the candidate's fit for the role and your team. Whether you lean toward compassion or command, evaluating the candidate's potential and proven performance is essential. And don't forget the cardinal rule: Never hire from a candidate pool of one. I have broken this rule, but it's always best to look at many resumes, narrow that group to 10 or fewer, do phone interviews and follow up with in-office interviews of at least two candidates.

1. **What Type of Worker Are They?**

    Ask candidates about their most significant career accomplishments and dig into the details to assess this. Their ability to speak confidently and in-depth about their achievements indicates their level of involvement and the impact they've made.

2. **Are They of Good Character?**

    Unfortunately, not everyone in the workforce has integrity. To assess character, ask the candidate about their worst boss and the worst employee they've worked with. Their responses will reveal what they find objectionable and, by extension, what they value. Additionally, checking references is crucial in verifying their character and the opinions formed during the interview.

3. Verifying Your Opinions and Their Capabilities

The final step involves checking references and examining the candidate's work product. This can be done through reference checks, evaluating work samples, or giving the candidate a trial project.

The reference check is crucial. Grab the candidate's resume and ask for the names of their last two or three bosses at the companies they worked for. Make it their responsibility to ensure those bosses call and speak to you. If they can't make that happen, then you shouldn't make the hire. Over the years, I've talked with many bosses and other colleagues of candidates. My overall takeaway is that it's obvious when a candidate is truly outstanding. Former bosses often provide over-the-top endorsements, clarifying that you're dealing with someone exceptional.

I remember one conversation with a reference who told me they gave their toughest assignments and biggest problems to the candidate we interviewed. We hired that candidate for an entry-level sales role, and they eventually rose to a VP level. You should feel great about the candidate after talking to former bosses. Years ago, I was hiring for an industry-specific position. We had a lot of trouble coming up with candidates for this role. I wanted to fill this position as it was part of our top growth initiatives. We found a qualified candidate, and I happened to know someone who had worked closely with this person. I called my connection for a reference. All my connection kept saying was that "John is a good guy." Every time I pressed for more, I kept getting, "John is a good guy." We hired John. It was a mistake. John was a good guy. He was a Positive Non-performer. It took us years to sort that out. It's easy to make a mis-hire when you need to fill a role.

When evaluating job candidates, you want to "try it before you buy it." When I was a division president, we had a department with roughly 35 people that was particularly suited to giving potential hires a "try-out." We always brought people in and paid them to work one day for us. They could evaluate us, and we would assess them. We had huge success with this approach. I've got a current client who is also succeeding with this method. Obviously, this is hard to do with someone remote or who currently has a job, so we tried to give candidates who couldn't spend a day with us actual projects to work on. Be creative in trying to examine their work product. When we hired creative writers for our marketing department, we had candidates submit multiple examples of what they had written. When hiring for the technology team, it's common for tech teams to have a special meeting with the candidate to ask them challenging tech questions to assess their fitness in the tech space. Sometimes, we had specific problems in the departments we were hiring for, and we assigned these problems to the candidates to solve. While some candidates removed themselves from consideration when we got to this step, great candidates appreciated the thoroughness of the process.

I used to spend upwards of $1,000 on an employment screening test, which we then had a consultant interpret. We did this for several years, and one day, I asked, "Have we ever ruled anyone out after taking the test?" The answer was no. We only tested the candidate we wanted and tended to overlook any negative test results.

THE TEAM APPROACH: GATHERING DIVERSE PERSPECTIVES

Using a team approach to interviewing can bring diverse perspectives to your hiring process. When using a team approach, assign specific criteria to each interviewer and ask for a simple "yes," "no," or "maybe" regarding whether the candidate should be hired. While a "yes" doesn't guarantee hiring, a "no" or "maybe" often means the candidate isn't the right fit. Even if one interviewer gives a strong "yes," it's crucial to consider all responses, including your own. This process ensures that the decision is comprehensive and well-rounded, reflecting immediate needs and long-term growth potential.

THE HIDDEN RED FLAG

There are many obvious red flags during the hiring process. You can easily search online if you want to delve into them, but one less apparent is when someone says, "I've got a candidate who I think could work." In my experience, when we settle for someone we "thought" could work, they fail every time. If you or your team have reservations during the interview, it's a strong indicator that the candidate may not be the right fit. In general, I've found that if you and your team are not genuinely excited about the candidate, then you should not make the hire.

THE 30-DAY RULE

This is the litmus test for new hires who are individual contributors. I've seldom seen this fail. After a new person starts, if I hear great things about them in their first 30 days, this person has nearly always turned out to be a great hire. And if someone struggles during their first 30 days, that is a red flag that you made a mis-hire. The only exception to this is youth. I have hired some young and inexperienced people in the past who just needed guidance and time. But if you hire someone who is over 25 and they struggle in their first 30 days, then my money says you made a mis-hire.

Later in my career, I got involved in correcting and taking action on mis-hires. In one extreme instance, we terminated a mis-hire after only three days of employment. It was an extreme mis-hire; we could not live with this mistake. The employee had been unemployed before we hired them, so they didn't give up an opportunity to work for us. We gave them two weeks' pay upon departure, so we were fair. This employee had been a consultant for most of their career, so we didn't have prior employer references to check, and this was a mistake.

When I think back over my career, I find that most of the best new hires stood out by making a significant impact within their first or second week, which impressed me and the team. It's a bit like a new romantic relationship; it usually doesn't take long to know if things will work out.

Please keep in mind for future reference that the effectiveness of the 30-day rule varies by organizational level. Specifically, it becomes increasingly challenging to apply as you ascend the hierarchy. For instance, a department head or CEO will need more time to make a significant impact compared to a new customer success representative.

CREATE A GREAT BEGINNING

A great onboarding experience is essential to setting the right tone for new hires. I remember showing up for a new job only to discover that I didn't have a desk or chair. No one on the team, besides the manager who was not there, knew who I was or even that a new employee was starting that day. I waited an uncomfortable hour until my new manager showed up. Don't put your new people through that. The following short list covers the basics you should have organized for a new hire's first day:

- A clean and prepared workspace.
- An appointment with IT to get outfitted with the appropriate technology.
- A scheduled orientation and team lunch.
- Clear goals and expectations for the first few weeks.
- Scheduled weekly one-on-ones for the first four weeks.

By addressing the personal and professional aspects of onboarding, you ensure your new hire feels valued while understanding what is expected of them from day one.

READER TAKEAWAYS

1. **Balance Compassion and Command in Your Hiring Approach**: Recognize the value of blending compassion with command in hiring decisions. A compassionate approach allows you to see potential and foster growth, while a command-oriented style ensures that you hire someone who has appropriate experience and can deliver results in relatively short order.

2. **Diversify Hiring Sources**: Use a variety of hiring sources. While some may be more successful (Primary Sources), others

(Secondary Sources) can provide unexpected opportunities. Balancing your approach will tap into diverse talent pools.

3. **Thorough Evaluation Process**: Ask questions revealing a candidate's achievements and character. Review a candidate's work, consider having them come in for a paid trial day, or give them a paid project. Do the reference checks and talk to candidates' actual bosses.

4. **Be Wary of Red Flags**: Pay attention to red flags during the hiring process, especially the "hidden red flag," ensuring that the interview team feels great about the candidate rather than just lukewarm or "okay."

5. **Onboarding and Early Assessment**: Create a positive and structured onboarding experience. Remember the 30-day rule and assess new hires to ensure they adjust well and meet expectations.

CHAPTER EXERCISE

1. **Evaluate Your Current Hiring Sources**:

   o Review your current hiring sources. Make a list and categorize them as Primary or Secondary sources based on their past success rates and the quality of candidates they provide. Consider adding additional sources.

2. **Analyze Past Hiring Decisions**:

   o Reflect on your past hiring decisions. Identify successful hires and mis-hires. What sources did these candidates come from? What made them successful or not? Did you overlook red flags for mis-hires?

3. **Identify Additional Red Flags**:

   o Based on your experience, list common red flags you've encountered during the hiring process. Use research to familiarize yourself with common red flags.

4. **Develop an Improved Hiring Strategy**:

   o Schedule an annual hiring process review. Learn from each hire, both successful and unsuccessful. Make improvements during the year but formalize them during the yearly review.

5. **Create an Onboarding Plan**:

   o Draft an onboarding plan that ensures new hires integrate smoothly into your team. Include initial training, introductions, and early performance assessments.

A FINAL THOUGHT

The more energy you and your company invest in hiring, the better your results will be. As I pointed out at the start of the chapter, a candidate can look great on paper, produce a winning interview, and still be a "mis-hire." You can minimize these mis-hires by talking to candidates' former employers. Make sure you choose who you want to speak to, and remember to make it the candidate's responsibility to arrange that connection. In the next and final chapter, we have a brief wrap-up followed by a list of additional resources that I love and that will help you as you continue to build on your management skills.

CHAPTER 10
THE SIMPLE WAY TO LOOK AT THINGS

One of my favorite management quotes is from Colin Powell: "Great leaders [and managers] are almost always great simplifiers, who can cut through argument, debate, and doubt, to offer a solution everybody can understand." In honor of that quote, I offer you a thought as you move forward. As you likely know by now, things come at you fast in management roles, and you must make most of your decisions on the fly. When faced with the never-ending deluge of decisions, I advise you to use your values as your "North Star." Remember Chapter 4, "Creating Your Management Persona." Every decision you make further defines who you are and what you stand for as a manager. You have a set of core values. Honor those and be fair to the company and the employee. You'll stay on the right path, becoming a great manager who attracts and retains top talent—people who are loyal to you and may even follow you to new opportunities as your career grows. When you have people leave their current positions to join you in new adventures within your company or at new companies, you know you have created work environments where people thrive.

CONNECTING WITH ME

This was my first book, and I hope the insights I've shared will be of lasting value to you as you embark on your management journey. I would appreciate your feedback and would love to hear what resonated most with you or what you disagreed with. You can reach me at bill@careerpathing.co.

WORKING WITH ME

Beyond being an author, I'm a coach who's spent most of his career in the trenches. If you're a manager who wants to go beyond the practical guidelines outlined in this book or seek an experienced and confidential resource, contact me at bill@careerpathing.co for a consultation. I work with first-line managers and senior executives. I have a small private coaching practice, but I can occasionally accept a new client.

Here is a quote from a current client that I find especially gratifying: "I was just promoted to vice president. Bill is the first person I called. Without Bill's guidance over the past year, I don't think that happens"—Debbie York.

You can check out more testimonials at careerpathing.co.

SPEAKING

I speak to companies and groups on multiple aspects of management and creating workforce engagement.

I'm currently working on a new presentation: "Shelve your side hustle and make your day job your passion." I related this to a personal experience in my own career. Email me, and we can discuss what my speaking to your group looks like.

YOUR OPPORTUNITY

You have the opportunity to impact people's lives every day. Very few things in life are as important to people as their jobs. No position within a company influences a person's work life more than a person's direct manager. The lessons and skills you read about and will now apply will significantly impact everyone on your team and, in turn, your career. It will be exciting and challenging. I believe that we must grow into great managers and leaders because we have been entrusted with responsibility for the work lives of others. I wish you great luck and big success as you continue to learn and grow in your career.

—Bill

ADDITIONAL RESOURCES

This list of resources is the current highlight reel from my personal collection. I love all of these resources. They have influenced my thinking and helped shape who I became as a manager and leader. If my book resonated with you, I'm confident these additional resources will too.

The CEO Next Door by Elena L. Botelho and Kim R. Powell with Tahl Raz

This excellent book boils down to how most leaders reach the CEO level and details their critical leadership attributes against a backdrop of showing the various paths leaders take to achieve their goal of becoming a CEO.

A Leadership Primer by Colin Powell, General, U.S. Army (Ret), former Chairman of the Joint Chiefs of Staff and former U.S. Secretary of State

You can find This PowerPoint presentation by typing "A Leadership Primer by Colin Powell" into your search engine. This PowerPoint presentation has 18 slides. Each slide contains a single lesson. For example, Lesson 2 starts with: "The day soldiers stop bringing you their problems is the day you have stopped leading them." I've been referring to this presentation for years, and I'm sure you noticed that I opened this final chapter with his quote, which came from this document.

Emotional Vampires by Albert J. Bernstein, PhD

Occasionally, you may encounter an employee, boss, or peer whose behavior is outside the bounds of normal behavior. This is the person everyone in the organization is always talking about, trying to "figure out." in my experience, this individual often has a personality disorder. While not a mental illness, it's closely related and helps explain what nobody has been able to figure out. I wish I had discovered this book earlier in my career because it answered many questions. The book outlines multiple personality disorders and has easy-to-follow checklists for an amateur diagnosis.

Creativity, Inc. by Ed Catmull with Amy Wallace

Ed, the President of Pixar Animation and Disney Animation, is considered the father of computer-generated animation. His team created *Toy Story*, the groundbreaking first entirely computer-generated feature film. In addition to telling the incredible story of how he invented computer-generated animation, the book has several chapters on management and leadership. It's filled with original insights I've not seen from any other source. I have always appreciated original thinking, and a book written by the creator of computer animation certainly delivers that. In Chapter 5, he makes an interesting distinction between candor and honesty, explaining when it's appropriate to be candid and when being completely forthright is actually the wrong approach. I've never seen anyone else take that position before.

Team Reconstruction: Building a High-Performance Work Group During Change by Price Pritchett and Ron Pound

I regularly use the principles in this 27-page booklet in my coaching practice. The premise is that the organization is generally paralyzed by fear and inertia during change. A void exists that screams for leadership. During times like these, managers need to shelve their fear and take charge. I came across this resource fairly early in my senior management tenure. I enjoyed the benefits of following its advice, and as I mentioned, I still use its principles to advise others.

Managing by Harold Geneen

This book is 40 years old but contains some classic advice. One of my favorite quotes from Chapter 14 is: "I think it is an immutable law in business that words are words, explanations are explanations, promises are promises, but only performance is reality. Performance alone is the best measure of your confidence, competence, and courage. Only performance gives you the freedom to grow as yourself. Just remember that performance is your reality. Forget everything else. That is why my definition of a manager is what it is: one who turns in the performance. No alibis to others or to oneself will change that. And when you have performed well, the world will remember it when everything else is forgotten. And, most importantly, so will you."

Friction EQ at gobeyond.com

As I mentioned in Chapter 5, Friction EQ, at www.gobeyond.work, is an amazingly quick, easy, and affordable stress behavior profile assessment that you can use to help you and your team better understand individual team members' stress responses.

Making Yourself Indispensable by John H. Zenger, Joseph R. Folkman, and Scott K. Edinger in the October 2011 Harvard Business Review

This terrific article identifies 16 leadership strengths and backs it up with extensive research. It shows that leaders who develop as few as two of these strengths into the 90th percentile can perform in almost the top quartile for overall leadership effectiveness. Those with four outstanding leadership traits rank in the top 10% of all leaders. The article also outlines a process for selecting strengths that align with your personal goals and company's needs and offers clear guidance on improving these strengths.